Sew Magical for Kids

Vice President and Chief Operations Officer: Tom Siebenmorgen
Vice President, Sales and Marketing: Pam Stebbins
Vice President, Operations: Jim Dittrich
Editor in Chief: Susan White Sullivan
Director of Designer Relations: Debra Nettles
Senior Art Director: Rhonda Shelby
Senior Prepress Director: Mark Hawkins

Produced for Leisure Arts, Inc. by Penn Publishing Ltd.
www.penn.co.il
Editor: Shoshana Brickman
Design and layout: Ariane Rybski
Photography by: Roee Fainburg
Illustrations: Laura Lee Burch
Technical editors: Tamara Bostwick, Rita Greenfeder

PRINTED IN CHINA

ISBN 9781574863291
Library of Congress Control Number: 2010927399

Cover photography by Roee Fainburg

Sew Magical for Kids

by

LAURA LEE BURCH

A LEISURE ARTS PUBLICATION

Contents

Introduction

My first book, **Sew Magical for Baby** was about making beautiful things for babies and toddlers, things a new baby needs and projects to help entertain babies and toddlers. Those projects were inspired by experiences with my own children.

My children aren't babies anymore and their toddler years are behind us, so I started thinking of new beautiful things to make for them, and more age appropriate ways to entertain them. I've put this collection of "big kid" toys in my new book, **Sew Magical for Kids**. My girls like to play make-believe games like dress-up, movie star, pirate ship, house, school and they LOVE to put on shows for us. I love listening to them play—they say the funniest things!

I think giving kids toys that stimulate their imaginations—toys like a cloth microphone, a big pirate ship or a stick horse—helps their creativity develop and expand. I always encourage their make-believe play, and encourage this type of wholesome activity over watching T.V. or sitting at the computer. I know these imaginative toys are good for my children (and my inner child loves them too!)

A Bit About Me

Because life is a journey, my creative story has changed over the years. Initially, I was a graphic designer and illustrator in Chicago. After moving to Israel, I started sewing many things for my girls out of necessity; this led to my opening a children's boutique full of my handmade creations. The next step in my journey was developing my website and blog (www.lauraleeburch.com) and teaching needle-felting classes.

Acknowledgements

I would like to thank the very talented Renana Una and Natalia Sohovolski, for assisting me in creating. Thank you to my cute models: my daughters, Emili and Elli Levitas, Janet Ewonkem, Ilan Cattaneo, and his brother, Maxi Schmutz. Thank you to my oldest daughter Lili for helping me with everything concerning the computer and for letting me bounce ideas off of her, and to my husband Doron for being my biggest fan.

Laura Lee Burch

Before You Start

Embroidery Stitches

Satin Stitch

This smooth, decorative stitch is good for making noses on stuffed animals (Figure A).

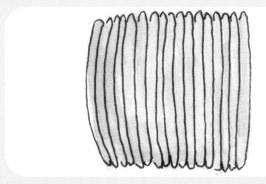

Figure A

Running stitch

This fast, in/out stitch makes straight lines (Figure B).

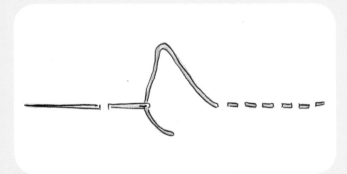

Figure B

Blanket stitch

This decorative stitch is sewn along fabric edges to prevent fraying.

STEP 1

Knot thread and bring needle up through fabric.

STEP 2

Make a small stitch, perpendicular to the edge of your project (Figure C).

Figure C

STEP 3

Start sewing about ¼" (0.6 cm) away from the edge, and stitch down.

STEP 4

Make sure loose part of thread is under the needle as you pull the stitch through the fabric (Figures D and E).

Figure D

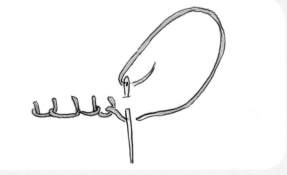

Figure E

Chain stitch

STEP 1

To start, bring the knotted thread up through the bottom of the fabric.

STEP 2

Put the needle into the fabric at A, bring the needle up at B (Figure F).

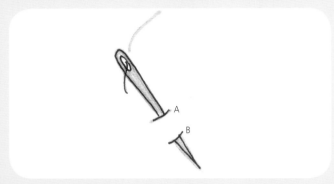

Figure F

STEP 3

Pull the thread under the needle, continue to pull the needle and thread through the fabric (Figure G).

Figure G

STEP 4

To start the next loop, put the needle into the fabric right after the finished loop (Figure H).

Figure H

French knot

This stitch is excellent for making eyes and for adding a decorative touch.

STEP 1

Knot thread and bring needle up through fabric.

STEP 2

Pull needle halfway through fabric at spot where you want French knot.

STEP 3

Wrap thread around the needle 6 or 7 times.

STEP 4

Pull needle rest of the way through fabric and wrapped embroidery thread, keeping thread together with your fingers.

STEP 5

Once needle has been pulled through fabric and thread has been wrapped around needle, keep pulling thread with needle until wrapped thread knots to form a small ball (Figure I).

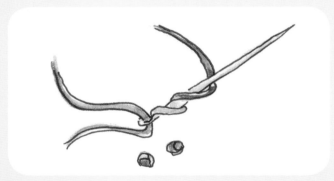

Figure I

Backstitch

This simple stitch goes from right to left and can be used to make the lines of a smile on a stuffed animal's face.

STEP 1

Knot thread and bring needle up through fabric. Make a stitch.

STEP 2

From backside of fabric, poke needle through fabric, ahead of first stitch, at approximately the same length as the first stitch.

STEP 3

Complete second stitch by placing needle at beginning of first stitch.

STEP 4

Continue in this manner to make a line (Figure J).

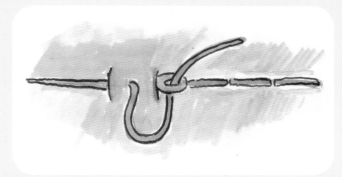

Figure J

Non-Embroidery Stitches

Slipstitch

This is used to close openings.

STEP 1

Knot thread and bring needle up through fabric. Make a small stitch through folded edge of fabric.

STEP 2

Make another stitch through folded edge of fabric, on other side. Continue sewing from one side to the other (Figure K). Stitches should be very hard to see.

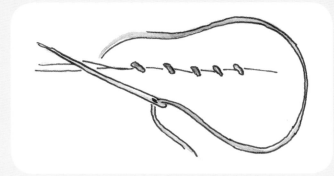

Figure K

Tips

- Always work with unwrinkled fabric.
- All seam allowances should be the width of the presser foot, unless otherwise instructed.
- After sewing curved seams, make several small snips on wrong side edge of fabric, along seam at curves. Take care not to cut stitches.
- Always trim corners before turning projects right side out.
- If possible, leave openings for stuffing objects or for turning them right side out in an area where you'll be adding something else, or along a straight edge that is easy to slipstitch closed.
- Use the sewing machine setting that is right for the fabric you are sewing. When sewing tricot, set your sewing machine for sewing stretchy fabrics. This allows fabric to stretch without the stitches breaking during play. When sewing vinyl, set machine stitch to a long width, since small stitches can make vinyl tear like a perforated piece of paper.

Experience Level

The row of krakens at the top of each project indicates the level of difficulty. One purple kraken indicates that the project is easy and just right for beginners; five purple krakens indicate that the project is challenging and more suitable for experienced sewers.

Getting Ready

Enlarging patterns

Many of the patterns in this book must be enlarged before tracing. You can do this at a photocopy shop, or on some home printers. If the required enlargement is too big for your printer (for example, if the pattern must be enlarged by 400%, and your printer's maximum is 200%) enlarge and print the pattern at 200%, then enlarge the printed pattern by another 200%.

Tracing patterns

Use a fabric pen or tailor's chalk to trace pattern pieces (Figure L).

Figure L

Laying out pattern pieces

• Many projects require the same pattern piece cut twice, once in reverse. In such cases, I recommend folding the fabric before you copy the pattern and cut. This makes it easier to produce identical pieces, and means you spend less time cutting the fabric.

• Some patterns have arrows that indicate how to lay pattern pieces on the fabric. This is important in fabrics with visible fibers, such as tricot and fleece.

• The bias is the diagonal line across the fabric. Fabrics cut on the bias are stretchier and drape well. Bias strips are used for binding fabric edges.

• The selvage is the area of fabric along the edges of both sides of a fabric roll. When laying out a pattern, the arrows on the pattern should be aligned with the selvage (Figure M).

Figure M

Using an iron

Make sure your fabric is flat before it is cut and sewn together. If necessary, iron the fabric before cutting it. You'll also need an iron (Figure N) for the following purposes:

Figure N

• To iron fabric stabilizer onto the back of fabrics.

• To press darts. Press these on a sleeve board rather than a flat ironing board to achieve the desired curve.

• To press seams. When making blankets and other flat pieces, it is often necessary to press seams open.

• To press finished pieces.

• To steam delicate fabrics. In such cases, you'll need to use a steam iron (Figure O).

• To flatten vinyl. Always use a pressing cloth so that you don't melt the vinyl.

Figure O

Basic Techniques

Finishing edges

The raw edges of most pieces of fabric will ravel unless they are secured in some way. To finish fabric edges, you can do one of the following:

STEP 1

Sew edges using a special sewing machine called a serger.

STEP 2

Sew edges on the zigzag setting with a regular sewing machine.

STEP 3

Cut edges with pinking shears. Fabrics with edges that do not ravel include felt, fleece, vinyl and leather.

Appliquéing shapes onto fabric

When sewing one piece of fabric onto another, the piece you appliqué should be slightly stiff. This prevents it from wrinkling when it is sewn onto the base fabric.

STEP 1

Iron fabric stabilizer onto back of piece you want to appliqué.

STEP 2

Pin appliqué firmly onto base piece. Make sure pins are placed vertically so that they can be sewn over.

STEP 3

Using the zigzag setting on your sewing machine (make the zigzag close together), sew around appliqué (Figure P). Press.

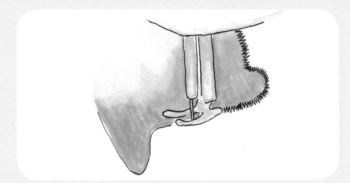

Figure P

Finishing seams with overstitch

This stitch is used to hold down unseen inner pieces and for decoration. It is also known as a topstitch (Figure Q).

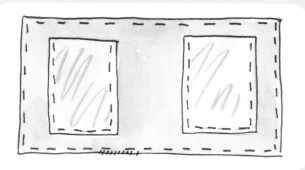

Figure Q

Making a simple hem

In many projects, you'll want to finish the edge and adjust the length by sewing a hem.

STEP 1

Make a ¼" (0.6 cm) fold along edge of fabric and iron it. Make a second ¼" (0.6 cm) fold and iron it.

STEP 2

Stitch folds closed near top fold. If you don't want the stitches to be seen, slipstitch the hem by hand (Figure R).

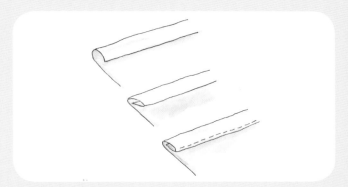

Figure R

Sewing pieces that will be turned right side out

Many projects are sewn together with their right sides facing. This enables a smooth seam when the connected pieces are turned right side out.

STEP 1

When sewing the seam, leave an opening for turning the project right side out.

STEP 2

After the project is sewn, make small cuts in the corners and curves. This makes the corners pointier and the curves smoother when the project is turned right side out. Be careful not to cut the seams (Figure S).

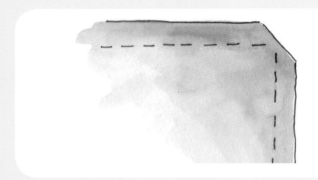

Figure S

STEP 3

Turn project right side out. Insert stuffing (if required), then hand sew the opening closed.

Sewing on bias tape

Bias tape is a strip of fabric that is folded and sewn over edges to give them a clean and decorative finish. Bias tape is cut on a 45° angle, making it stretchy and easy to fold along curves.

STEP 1

Trim the area where the bias tape will be sewn about ⅛" (0.3 cm) from the seam. Press open half of the bias tape, and line up the raw edge of the fabric with the unfolded side of the bias tape (Figure T).

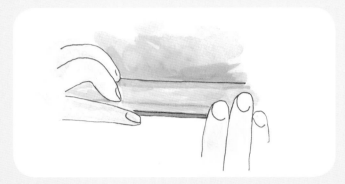

Figure T

STEP 2

Pin the right side of the bias tape to the right side of the fabric. Stitch the bias tape to the fabric, with a seam allowance equal to width of the presser foot (Figure U).

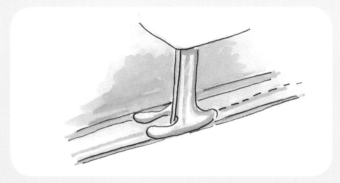

Figure U

STEP 3

Fold the bias tape in half so that it almost touches the edge of the object you are sewing.

STEP 4

Fold the bias tape over again so that it is folded over the edge of the fabric. Sew along the bias tape, near the outer edge (Figure V).

Figure V

STEP 5

To finish, cross the beginning and end pieces of bias tape, and sew down. Press.

Making shanks

A shank makes the area between two separate pieces stronger. Shanks are required in areas where a button is added to a garment, an arm is sewn onto a doll, or a wing is attached to a duck. To make a shank, do the following:

STEP 1

Insert a knotted piece of thread near the joint and make a small stitch.

STEP 2

Wrap the thread around the joint four or five times, then knot the thread and cut (Figure W).

Figure W

Making gathers and ruffles

Gathers can help one sewn piece fit into another (like a sleeve into a sleeve hole). Ruffles add an extra piece of gathered fabric, and make everything cuter!

STEP 1

Using heavy thread, sew two lines of wide stitches across the fabric edge. (Make three lines of wide stitches if the piece is very long.)

STEP 2

Each stitch consists of an upper and lower thread. Knot the thread on one side. Take the threads (top or bottom) on the other side and gently pull at the same time.

STEP 3

Gently adjust the gathers with your fingers, pulling them evenly across the fabric edge (Figure X).

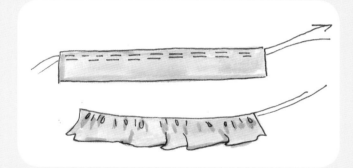

Figure X

Sewing pointed edges

Carefully snip pointed edges at regular intervals, so that when the fabric is turned right side out, the points are sharp. Take care not to cut the seam (Figure Y).

Figure Y

Sewing vinyl and foam

- Put a layer of sheer tissue paper over and under the vinyl (or foam) before sewing. The tissue paper allows the presser foot to slide over the vinyl (or foam), making an even stitch. Tear the paper away after you've finished sewing.
- Set your machine stitch to a long width since small stitches tend to cut the vinyl (or foam), making it tear like a perforated piece of paper at the line of stitching.
- Iron the vinyl (or foam) to eliminate wrinkles by placing a pressing cloth (a piece of cotton is fine) between the vinyl (or foam) and the iron. Don't leave the iron on the pressing cloth too long.
- Use a special plastic presser foot made for sewing vinyl (or foam) (Figure Z).

Figure Z

Stuffing sewn objects

When sewing an object that will be stuffed, leave a small opening along a straight area of the object's seam for inserting stuffing or batting.

STEP 1

Tuck the stuffing it into the opening and use a chopstick, dowel rod, or the end of a paintbrush to push the stuffing into the toy.

STEP 2

If there are arms, legs, or other appendages, stuff these first. Then stuff the head and body.

STEP 3

Continue stuffing the toy until it is firm to the touch. Slipstitch the opening to close. Press or steam, as instructed (Figure AA).

Figure AA

Designs

Little Ballerina Ballet Bag

When people see this ballet bag, they'll likely think it's a real ballerina outfit! The perfect accessory for any ballet-smitten girl who can't get enough pink tulle, this bag is just the right size for holding a pair of ballet slippers and leotard.

EXPERIENCE LEVEL

DIMENSIONS

• 11½" x 12" (29 cm x 30 cm) (without handles)

MATERIALS

• Decorative fabric (bodice center): 6" x 9" (15 cm x 23 cm)
• Iron-on fabric stabilizer (bodice center): 6" x 9" (15 cm x 23 cm)
• Pink satin (bodice, lining and handles): 19" x 21" (48 cm x 53 cm)
• Pink tulle (tutu): 3 pieces, each 5" x 40" (13 cm x 102 cm)
• Pink ribbon (optional handles): 2 pieces, each 18½" (47 cm)
• Velcro®: 1 piece, 1" x 1" (2.5 cm x 2.5 cm)
• Tiny fabric rose
• Matching thread

TOOLS

• Fabric pen
• Iron
• Pins
• Scissors
• Sewing machine

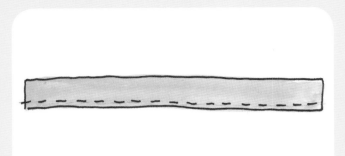

Figure A

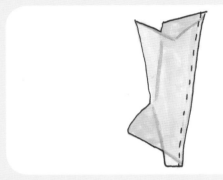

Figure B

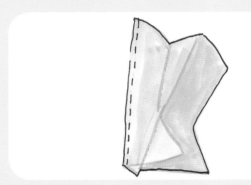

Figure C

Figure D

Getting Started

6 pattern pieces

- Copy the pattern pieces (page 102) and cut out.
- Iron fabric stabilizer onto the back of the decorative fabric.
- Trace the pattern pieces onto the fabric and cut.

Pink satin ribbons can be used for handles instead of sewn ones.

Use a special presser foot for gathering fabric for a faster way to prepare the tulle.

Instructions

Handles

STEP 1

Fold each handle piece in half lengthwise; press. Sew each handle together, right sides facing, along the long side (Figure A).

STEP 2

Turn the handles right sides out; press.

Bodice

STEP 3

Pin one bodice front/side piece to the bodice front/center piece, right sides facing; sew (Figure B). Press the seam open.

STEP 4

Pin the second side bodice piece to the center bodice piece, right sides facing; sew (Figures C and D). Press open.

STEP 5

Pin the bodice back piece to the front bodice, right sides facing; sew seams along the sides (Figure E). Turn right side out; press.

Lining

STEP 6

Pin the front and back lining pieces together, right sides facing. Sew the side seams, and sew in 1" (2.5 cm) from the corner on each side of the bottom, leaving an opening in the center (Figure F).

Figure E

Figure F

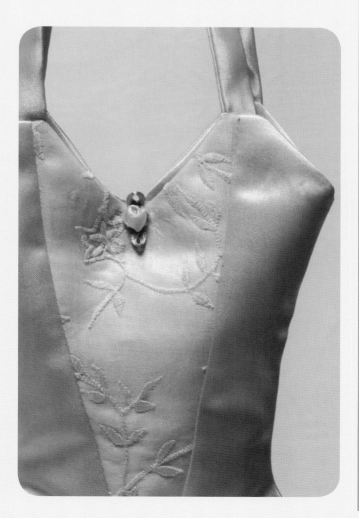

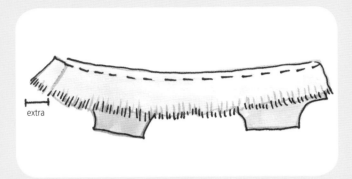

Figure G

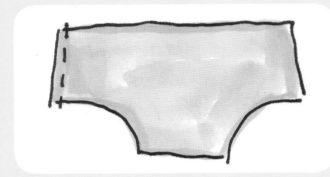

Figure H

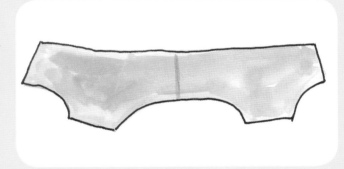

Figure I

Tutu

STEP 7

Gather each strip of tulle until it is about 6" (15 cm) long, which is about 1" (2.5 cm) wider than the panties (Figure G).

STEP 8

Pin both panty pieces together, right sides facing. Sew the seam along one side (Figure H); press open (Figure I).

STEP 9

Pin one gathered tulle strip across the pressed open panties, on the right side of the fabric, leaving about 1" (2.5 cm) of extra tulle on the right-hand side of the panties. When sewing the tulle in step 10, do not sew down this extra flap.

STEP 10

With the panties pressed open, on the right side of the fabric, sew as follows:

a. Sew the first layer of tulle at the bottom of the panties (Figure J).

b. Pin the second layer of tulle, upside down, directly above the first layer of tulle. Sew the tulle (Figure K), then flip it down (Figure L). (This makes the skirt fluffy.)

c. Pin the third layer of tulle directly above the second layer, at the top of the panties; sew (Figures M and N).

STEP 11

Fold the panties back together so that right sides are facing and the layers of tulle are sandwiched inside; pin. Sew the other side seam (Figure O).

STEP 12

Turn the panties right side out, and fold the extra 1" (2.5 cm) of tulle on all three layers over the seam; sew. This extra bit of tulle will hide the start/stop area, and make the line of tulle seamless (Figure P).

STEP 13

Turn the panties inside out; sew the crotch seam closed (Figure Q).

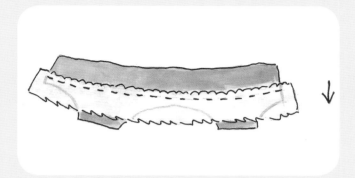

Figure J

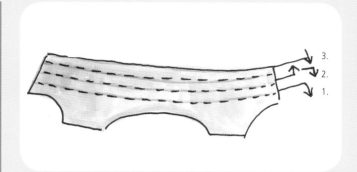

Figure N

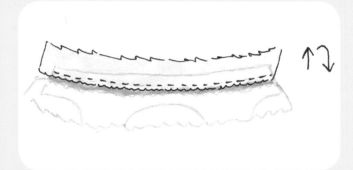

Figure K

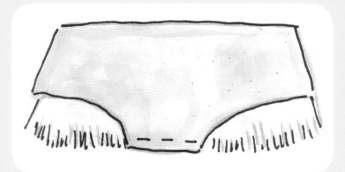

Figure O

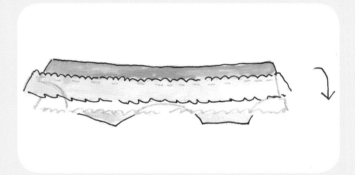

Figure L

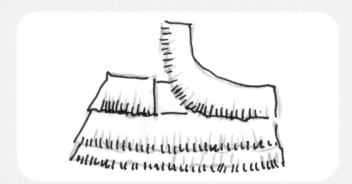

Figure P

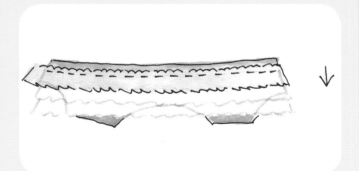

Figure M

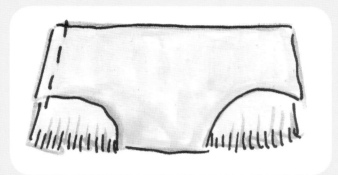

Figure Q

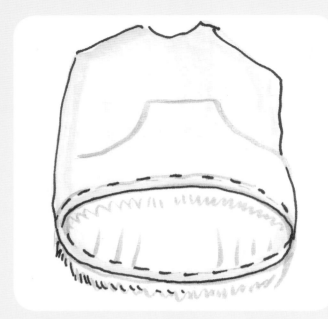

Figure R

Figure S

Attaching tutu to bodice

STEP 14

Turn the bodice wrong side out. Line up the waist of the bodice and the waist of the tutu and pin the tutu to the bodice, upside down and right sides facing. Sew around the waist (Figure R).

STEP 15

Turn right side out. The exterior bodice is now complete (Figure S).

STEP 16

Pin the handles on the front and back bodice so that they hang down; sew down each handle end.

Inserting lining

STEP 17

Put the bodice with the tutu into the lining, right sides facing, via the hole in the crotch lining; tuck in the handles. Line up the points at the top of the lining and bodice; pin. Sew all around the top (Figure T).

STEP 18

Sew back and forth across the handles to reinforce them.

STEP 19

Turn bag right side out, and fold in the edges of the interior crotch; sew closed. Stuff the lining into the bag.

STEP 20

Sew corresponding sides of Velcro® on the inside center of the bodice. Hand sew the rose at the top of the front bodice in the center (Figure U). Steam the tulle up, press the bag.

Figure T

Figure U

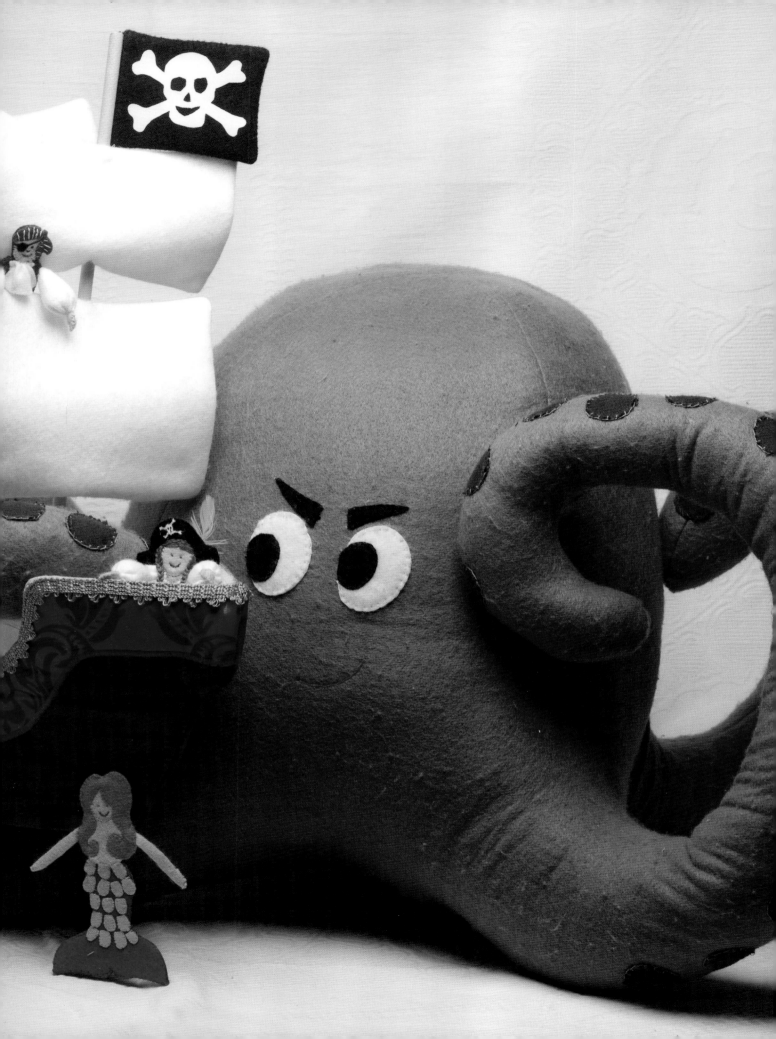

Fear the Kraken!

According to pirate lore, the Kraken dwells deep in Davy Jones' locker! This incredibly large sea monster, feared by pirates and other seafaring fellows, was believed to attack ships and drag sailors deep down to watery graves. This Kraken pillow is a lovable 'bad guy' for your children to play with.

EXPERIENCE LEVEL

DIMENSIONS

• 20" (51 cm) tall x 44" (112 cm) around x 42" (107 cm) wide

MATERIALS

• Light purple felt (body): 75" x 49" (191 cm x 124 cm)
• Iron-on fabric stabilizer (body): 75" x 49" (191 cm x 124 cm)
• Dark purple felt (tentacle dots): 17" x 8" (43 cm x 20 cm)
• White felt (eyes): 3" x 5" (7.5 cm x 13 cm)
• Black felt (eye pupils, eyebrows): 2½" x 5" (6 cm x 13 cm)
• Fabric glue
• Light purple, white, black and red embroidery thread
• Polyester fiberfill stuffing

TOOLS

• Chopstick
• Embroidery needle
• Iron
• Pins
• Scissors
• Sewing machine
• Tailor's chalk

Opposite: Fear the Kraken! (pages 25-27), Plundering Pirate Ship (pages 85-89), Mermaid Doll (pages 98-99), Pretty Pirate (pages 96-97) and First Mate (pages 94-95).

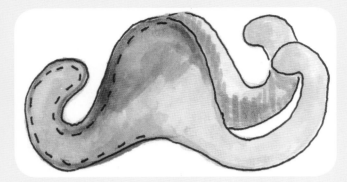

Figure A

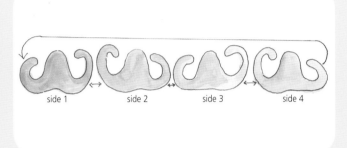

Figure B

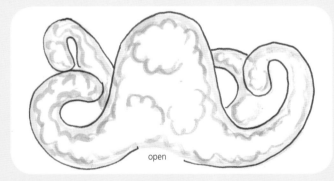

Figure C

Getting Started

6 pattern pieces

- Copy the pattern pieces (page 103) and cut out.
- Iron fabric stabilizer onto the light purple felt.
- Trace the pattern pieces onto the fabric and cut out.

Instructions

STEP 1

Pin together two side pieces, right sides facing. Sew together along one arm, from the notch on the bottom to the top center of the head (Figure A).

STEP 2

Pin the third side piece to one side of the first two pieces; sew along one arm, from the notch on the bottom to the top center of the head. Match the fourth side piece to the first and third pieces; sew seams along both sides (Figure B). The bottom will be open.

STEP 3

Turn right side out and begin to stuff firmly. Use small pieces of stuffing to fill the tips of the arms and pack the stuffing with a chopstick. Continue stuffing the kraken, paying special attention to the curved arms and packing firmly so that the arms are not wrinkly (Figure C).

STEP 4

Once the arms are stuffed, the bottom of the kraken will have a large square opening. Using embroidery thread, sew across the opening horizontally and vertically in a lacing pattern to reinforce the area (Figure D).

STEP 5

Pin the bottom piece over the laced opening; slipstitch all around to close the opening (Figure E).

STEP 6

Glue tentacle pieces on the underside of the kraken arms. Embroider around each tentacle with blanket stitch.

STEP 7

Glue each black eye piece onto a white eye piece. Embroider around the black eye pieces with blanket stitch. Glue the eyes onto one side of the kraken (see pattern). Embroider around the white eye piece with blanket stitch.

STEP 8

Glue the eyebrow pieces above the eyes and embroider around each one with blanket stitch. Embroider a mouth with backstitch (Figure F).

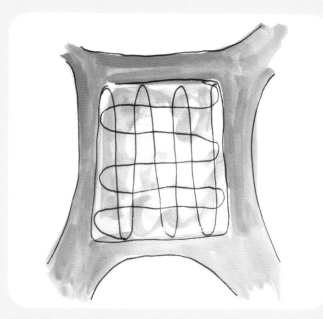

Figure D

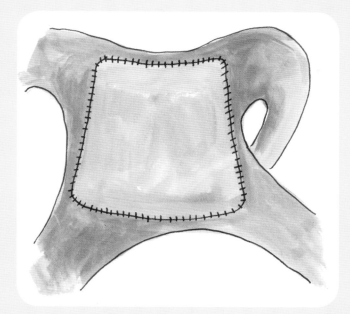

Figure E

Figure F

Superhero Cape and Mask

In my opinion, the cape is the single most important costume accessory. It can transform your child into a superhero or villain, vampire or magician, king or queen, knight or maiden. Adding a simple mask upgrades the outfit with ease! Create a variety of capes and masks, using different types and colors of fabric. To make different sizes, add or subtract 10" (25 cm) from the length.

EXPERIENCE LEVEL

DIMENSIONS

- Cape: 34" x 56" (86 cm x 142 cm)
- Mask: 30" x 3" (76 cm x 7.5 cm)

SIZE

- Suitable for ages 5 to 10
- To make small, subtract 10" (25 cm) from the length of the cape. Add 10" (25 cm) to the length to make size large.

MATERIALS

- Lycra® or satin (cape and mask): 42" x 75" (107 cm x 190 cm) [cape: (34" x 56") 86 cm x 142 cm; mask: 30" x 3" (76 cm x 7.5 cm)]
- Matching bias tape, ½" (1.2 cm) thick (for tying): 46" (117 cm)
- Decorative trim (optional)

TOOLS

- Fabric pen
- Iron
- Pins
- Scissors
- Sewing machine
- Tailor's chalk

Getting Started

2 pattern pieces

- Copy the pattern pieces (pages 104–105) and cut out.
- Trace the pattern pieces onto the fabric and cut out.

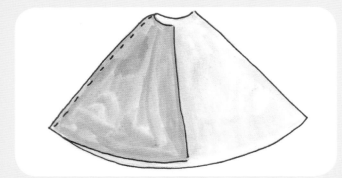

Figure A

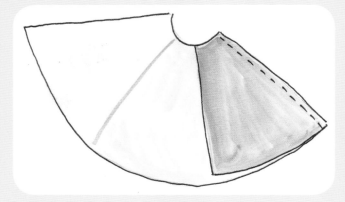

Figure B

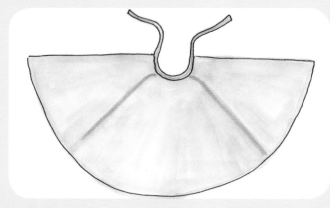

Figure C

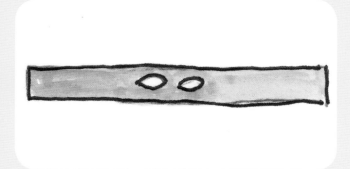

Figure D

Instructions

Cape

STEP 1

Pin one side piece onto the back piece, right sides facing; sew along the straight edge (Figure A).

STEP 2

Pin the other side piece onto the back piece, right sides facing; sew along the straight edge (Figure B).

STEP 3

Over-lock or zigzag the side seams and bottom of the cape.

STEP 4

Hem the sides and bottom of the cape.

STEP 5

Pin bias tape along the neckline of the cape, leaving an extra 15 " (38 cm) on each side for tying; sew (Figure C).

STEP 6

Pin decorative trim along the sides, bottom and/or neck of the cape (optional); hand sew.

Mask

STEP 7

Trim mask piece to fit. If using fabric other than Lycra®, over-lock or zigzag the edges and eye holes (Figure D).

Ahoy! It's a Pirate Hat

Sometimes, the only thing you need to feel like a pirate is a really good accessory. And aside from the standard eye patch, no accessory is quite as recognizable as the favorite Pirate Hat. With this simple-to-sew pirate hat perched on your child's head, they'll be all set for smooth sailing into the world of buccaneers.

EXPERIENCE LEVEL

DIMENSIONS

• 14" x 8" (36 cm x 20 cm)

SIZE

• Suitable for ages 4 to 6

MATERIALS

• Black felt (hat): 20½" x 22½" (52 cm x 57 cm)

• White cotton (appliqué): 3" x 4" (7.5 cm x 10 cm)

• Double-sided iron-on fabric stabilizer (appliqué): 3" x 4" (7.5 cm x 10 cm)

• White bias tape, ½" (1.2 cm) thick (trim): 50" (127 cm)

TOOLS

Tools

• Fabric pen

• Iron

• Pins

• Scissors

• Sewing machine

• Tailor's chalk

Getting Started

4 pattern pieces

• Copy the pattern pieces (page 106) and cut out.

• Iron fabric stabilizer onto the back of the white cotton.

• Trace the pattern pieces onto the fabric and cut out.

Figure A

Figure B

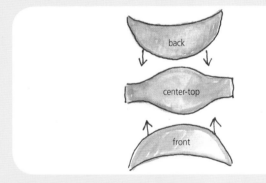

Figure C

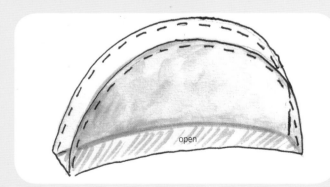

Figure D

Instructions

STEP 1

Iron the appliqué piece onto the center of the front brim piece (Figure A).

STEP 2

Pin the front and back brim pieces together, right sides facing; sew together along the straight bottom edges (Figure B).

STEP 3

Pin one side piece to the center piece; sew along rounded side (Figure C). Pin the other side piece to the center piece; sew (Figure D).

STEP 4

Pin the brim front (with skull) to the side front and the brim back to the side back; sew around the base of the hat (Figure E). Flip the brim up.

STEP 5

Pin bias tape all around the edge of the brim; sew. To keep the brim facing upward, sew together the front and back of the brim 2" (5 cm) from the right and left sides. This prevents the brim from flopping down, and helps hold the shape of the hat.

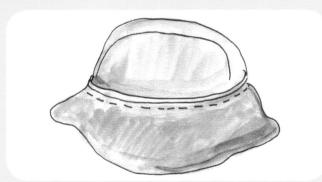

Figure E

Opposite: Ahoy! It's a Pirate Hat (pages 31-32) and Jolly Roger Pirate Flag (pages 34-35).

Jolly Roger Pirate Flag

In the olden days, after pirates took over a ship, the new ship was used to attack other ships. Just before attacking the next ship, the pirates would raise their intimidating flag. This Jolly Roger isn't scary, but it is perfect for fueling your child's imagination. Hang it over your child's bed to give the entire room a swashbuckling and adventurous pirate feeling.

EXPERIENCE LEVEL

DIMENSIONS

• 29" x 17¾" (74 cm x 45 cm)

MATERIALS

• Black felt (flag): 29½" x 18" (75 cm x 46 cm)
• White felt (skull and crossbones appliqué): 22" x 14" (56 cm x 36 cm)
• Red and white striped cotton fabric (bandana appliqué): 14" x 7" (36 cm x 18 cm)
• Iron-on fabric stabilizer (flag, appliqués): 60" x 30" (152 cm x 76 cm)
• White, red and black embroidery thread

TOOLS

• Embroidery needle
• Fabric pen
• Iron
• Pins
• Scissors
• Sewing machine
• Tailor's chalk

Getting Started

3 pattern pieces

- Copy the pattern pieces (page 107) and cut out.
- Iron fabric stabilizer onto the back of all of the fabrics.
- Trace the pattern pieces and cut out.

Instructions

STEP 1

Pin the skull and crossbones appliqué piece onto the front flag piece (see pattern; sew all around the appliqué (Figure A).

STEP 2

Pin the bandana appliqué piece onto the front flag piece (see pattern); sew all around the appliqué (Figure B).

STEP 3

Embroider around the eye sockets, nose, mouth and bandana with blanket stitch.

STEP 4

Pin together the front and back flag pieces, wrong sides facing, and sew all around.

Figure A

Figure B

Excalibur Sword

Excalibur was the magical sword of the legendary, mythical King Arthur. This playful replica is quick to inspire stories featuring King Arthur and his Knights, as well as Merlin the Magician, the Lady of the Lake, Lancelot, Guinevere, castles, battles, medieval love, and more.

EXPERIENCE LEVEL

DIMENSIONS

• 30" x 9" (76 cm x 23 cm)

MATERIALS

• Silver vinyl or satin (blade): 7" x 25" (18 cm x 64 cm)
• Iron-on fabric stabilizer (blade, if using satin): 7" x 25" (18 cm x 64 cm)
• Black vinyl (handle): 7" x 18" (18 cm x 46 cm)
• Gray thread
• Thin craft plastic (blade reinforcement) 7" x 25" (18 cm x 64 cm)
• Dowel rod (blade reinforcement): ¼" x 29" (0.6 cm x 74 cm)
• Polyester fiberfill stuffing
• 2 faux jewels

TOOLS

• Fabric glue
• Fabric pen
• Iron
• Pins
• Pressing cloth
• Scissors
• Sewing machine
• Tailor's chalk

Opposite: Superhero Cape (pages 29-30), Excalibur Sword (pages 37-29) and Knight's Hood (pages 40-43).

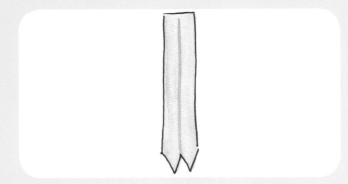

Figure A

Figure B

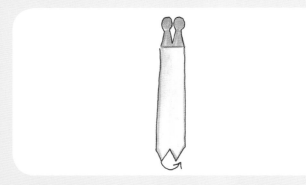

Figure C

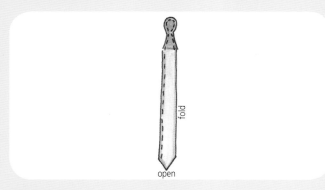

Figure D

Getting Started

4 pattern pieces

- Copy the pattern pieces (page 108) and cut out.
- Iron fabric stabilizer onto the back of the satin fabric, if using.
- Trace the pattern pieces onto the fabric and plastic and cut out.

Instructions

STEP 1

Line up the straight edge of the blade exterior piece with the straight edge of the handle pieces, right sides facing. Sew across the straight edge of the handle pieces (Figures A and B).

STEP 2

Press the handles up, then fold in half, right sides facing (Figure C).

STEP 3

Leaving the blade tip open, sew the left side of the blade and around the handle (Figure D). Turn right side out; press.

STEP 4

Slide the plastic blade interior pieces into the opening at the tip of the blade (Figure E). Slide the dowel rod between the blade interior pieces (Figure F).

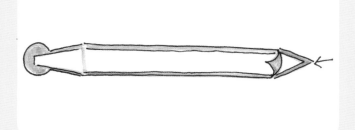

Figure E

STEP 5

Slipstitch the end of the blade to close.

STEP 6

Pin the cross guard pieces together, right sides facing. Sew together, leaving the center top and bottom part open (Figure G). Turn right side out.

STEP 7

Slide the cross guard onto the handle (Figure H), drawing it up until the bottom of the blade. Stuff the left and right sides of the handle with stuffing (Figure I); slipstitch the center handle to close.

STEP 8

Glue or stitch jewels onto either side of the handle (Figure J).

Figure F

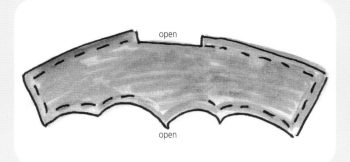

Figure G

Figure H

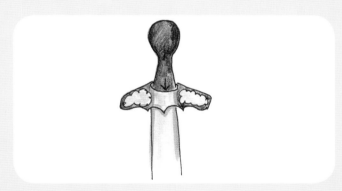

Figure I

Figure J

Noble Knight's Hood

Does your child aspire to be a valiant knight? If so, then regular practice in slaying dragons and rescuing people in distress is a must! This noble hood will protect your little knight in any battle he or she faces. Pair the hood with a silver cape (page 28) and Excalibur the Sword (page 36) for a truly invincible knight's costume.

EXPERIENCE LEVEL

DIMENSIONS

• 18" x 15" (46 cm x 38 cm)

MATERIALS

• Silver satin (hood, collar and nose guard): 43" x 38" (109 cm x 97 cm)
• Red felt (trim): 44" x 4" (112 cm x 10 cm)
• Gray thread
• Velcro®: 1 piece, 2" x 1" (5 cm x 2.5 cm)

TOOLS

• Fabric pen
• Iron
• Pins
• Scissors
• Sewing machine
• Tailor's chalk

Getting Started

5 pattern pieces

- Copy the pattern pieces (pages 109–110) and cut out.
- Trace the pattern pieces onto the fabric and cut out.

Instructions

Trim

STEP 1

Pin the trim piece to the outer edge of one collar piece, with the jagged edge of the trim facing in (Figure A).

STEP 2

Pin the other collar piece on top, so that the right sides of the collar pieces are facing and the trim piece is sandwiched between them.

STEP 3

Sew together around the outer edge and both straight edges of the collar piece (Figure B).

STEP 4

Turn right side out; press (Figure C).

Hood

STEP 5

Pin the outer front hood pieces together, right sides facing; sew together along the top seam (Figure D). Repeat with the lining front hood pieces. Press the seams open.

Figure A

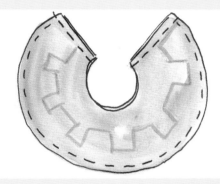

Figure B

Figure C

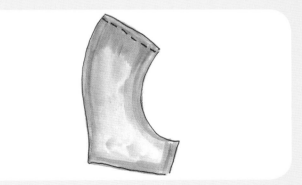

Figure D

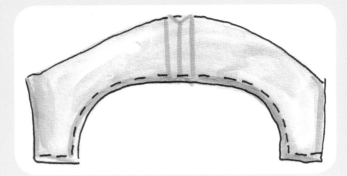

Figure E

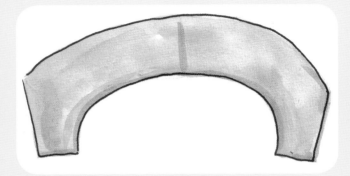

Figure F

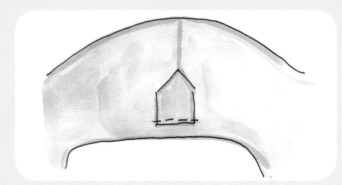

Figure G

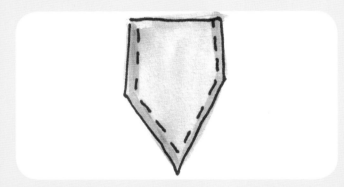

Figure H

Open the outer and lining hood; pin together, right sides facing; sew along the inside curved edge (Figure E). Turn right side out, press (Figure F).

Nose guard

STEP 7

Pin the nose guard pieces together, right sides facing. Sew around the shape, leaving the top open (Figure G). Turn right side out; press.

STEP 8

Pin the nose guard to the front center of the hood, ¾" (2 cm) from the edge, with the point facing the back of the hood. Sew along the open end of the nose guard (Figure H).

STEP 9

Fold the nose guard down toward the front and sew along the sides, close to the edges.

Hood

STEP 10

Pin the back hood pieces together, right sides facing. Sew the back seam (Figure I), then over-lock or zigzag the back seam. Turn right side out; press.

STEP 11

Pin the back hood pieces to the front hood pieces, matching notches, right sides facing. Sew along the side seams, then over-lock or zigzag the side seams. Turn right side out; press (Figures J and K).

STEP 12

Pin the collar piece to the hood piece, right sides facing, matching the bottom hood seam to the inner neck seam. The finished edges of the front hood and collar piece should line up (Figure L). Sew together then over-lock or zigzag the seam; press.

STEP 13

Pin corresponding sides of Velcro® onto the corners of the front of the hood (see pattern); sew (Figure M).

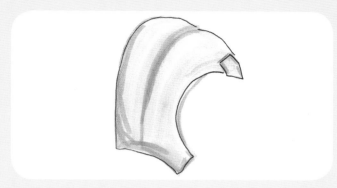

Figure K

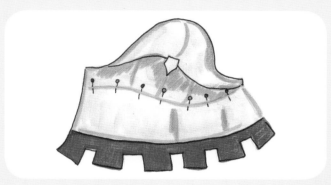

Figure L

Figure I

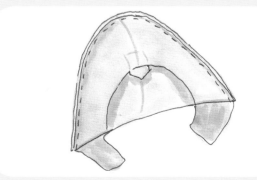

Figure J

Figure M

43

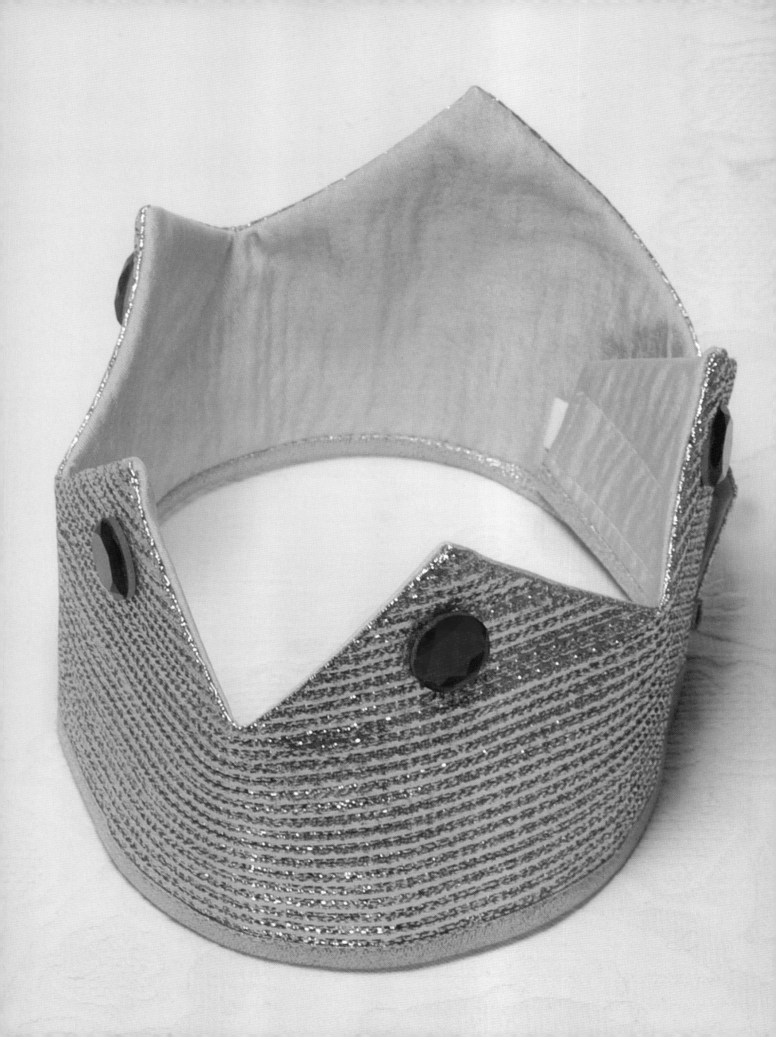

A Royal Crown

Crowns and capes go together like peanut butter and jam, sugar and spice, bagels and cream cheese. Top this crown with some fancy faux gems and match it with a gold cape (see page 28) for a really royal look. The design is comfortable to wear and easy to adjust thanks to the Velcro® fastener. To make an even smaller crown possible, use a longer piece of Velcro®.

EXPERIENCE LEVEL

SIZE

• Suitable for ages 6 to 8

DIMENSIONS

• 25" x 4¾" (63 cm x 12 cm)

MATERIALS

• Decorative fabric: 10" x 29" (25 cm x 74 cm)
• Satin (lining): 10" x 29" (25 cm x 74 cm)
• Iron-on fabric stabilizer, heavy weight: 10" x 29" (25 cm x 74 cm)
• Velcro®: 1 piece, 2" x 1" (5 cm x 2.5 cm)
• Matching thread
• Faux jewels, crystals or beads
• Decorative trim (optional): 29" (74 cm)

TOOLS

• Fabric pen
• Iron
• Needle
• Pins
• Scissors
• Sewing machine
• Tailor's chalk

Getting Started

1 pattern piece

• Copy the pattern piece (page 111) and cut out.
• Iron fabric stabilizer onto the back of the decorative fabric.
• Trace the pattern piece onto the fabric and cut out.

Figure A

Figure B

Figure C

Figure D

Instructions

STEP 1

Pin both crown pieces together, right sides facing. Sew around the entire shape, leaving an opening along the bottom straight edge (Figure A).

STEP 2

To reduce bulk and make turning easier, trim the point tips along the top of the crown and clip into the seam allowances of the inside points (do not cut through the seam) (Figure B). Turn right side out and slipstitch the opening to close; press.

STEP 3

Pin corresponding sides of Velcro® onto each end of the crown (see pattern); sew (Figure C).

STEP 4

Glue or sew the faux jewels, crystals or beads onto the crown. Pin decorative trim around the base of the crown (optional); sew (Figure D).

Broomstick Stallion

As a child, I remember spending hours with my sister riding horses made from old mops around our backyard. Sometimes we were cowgirls, sometimes we were soldiers, sometimes we were just girls with our own horses. This broomstick horse can be the base for many adventures. Needless to say, it requires much less upkeep than a real horse!

EXPERIENCE LEVEL

DIMENSIONS

• 49" x 16" (124 cm x 41 cm)

MATERIALS

• Red vinyl (horse): 40" x 19" (102 cm x 48 cm)
• Foam (horse): 40" x 19" (102 cm x 48 cm)
• Red fringe (mane): 24" (61 cm)
• Blue ribbon (harness): 83" (211 cm)
• Blue embroidery thread
• Red velvet (stick cover): 3" x 33" (7.5 cm x 84 cm)
• Broomstick: 3" x 47" (7.5 cm x 120 cm)
• 2 doll eyes with fasteners
• Polyester fiberfill stuffing
• Fabric glue
• Red and blue thread

TOOLS

• Embroidery needle
• Fabric pen
• Iron
• Pins
• Pressing cloth
• Scissors
• Sewing machine

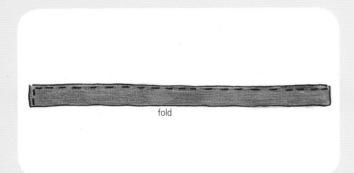

fold

Figure A

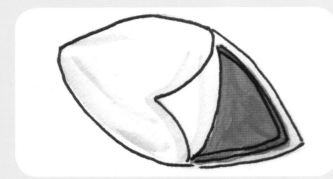

Figure B

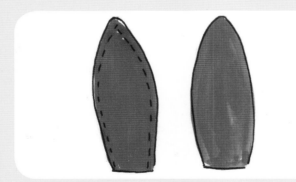

Figure C

Getting Started

2 pattern pieces

- Copy the pattern pieces (page 112) and cut out.
- Trace the pattern pieces onto the fabric and foam and cut out.

> To make it easier to sew the vinyl, use a presser foot for vinyl.

Instructions

Broomstick

STEP 1

Fold the velvet in half lengthwise, right sides facing. Sew along one short and one long side (Figure A).

STEP 2

Turn right side out and slide onto the broomstick.

Head

STEP 3

Pin pairs of ear pieces together, right sides facing (foam, vinyl, vinyl, foam) (Figure B).

STEP 4

Sew around each ear, leaving the bottom open. Turn ears right side out; press (Figure C).

STEP 5

Cut slits in each head piece (see pattern). Fold each ear in half lengthwise and insert into slit, facing forward.

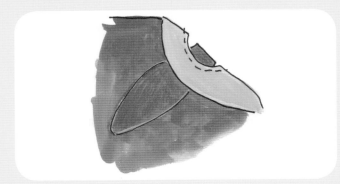

Figure D

Figure E

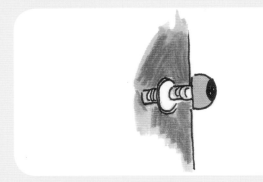

Figure F

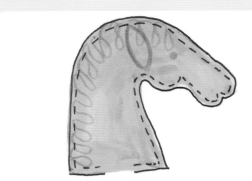

Figure G

STEP 6

Fold over the top of each head piece and sew across the bottom of the ear (the part sticking out of the underside of the slit) (Figure D). Pin the fringe onto the right side of one head piece, along the top; sew (Figure E).

STEP 7

Poke a very small hole in each head piece (see pattern). Insert one doll eye into each hole and secure by twisting the fasteners onto the back of each eye (Figure F).

STEP 8

Pin the head pieces together, right sides facing (foam, vinyl, fringe, vinyl, foam). Sew from notch to notch, leaving the bottom open (Figure G).

STEP 9

Turn right side out and press using a pressing cloth.

STEP 10

Stuff the head firmly by pushing several handfuls of stuffing into the top. Insert the broomstick, then insert more stuffing all around the broomstick (Figure H).

STEP 11

Slipstitch the bottom of the horse head to close.

Harness

STEP 12

Cut the ribbon into 4 pieces: 12" (30 cm) for the nose (a); 41" (104 cm) for the reigns (b); 21" (53 cm) for the ears (c); 9" (23 cm) for the forehead (d).

STEP 13

Wrap ribbon a (Figure I) around the horse's nose and sew the ends together (Figure J).

STEP 14

Pin both ends of ribbon b onto ribbon a, one end on each side of the horse's face (Figures K and L).

STEP 15

Pin both ends of ribbon c onto ribbon a, in the same place as ribbon b. Sew all three ribbons together (Figure M).

STEP 16

Fit the ribbon harness onto the horse (Figure N). Place ribbon d across the horse's forehead, and pin the ends onto either side of ribbon b. Hand sew ribbon d onto ribbon b (Figure O).

Figure H

Figure L

Figure I

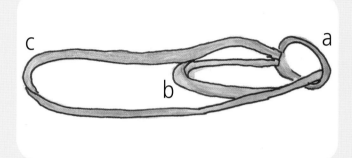

Figure M

Figure J

Figure N

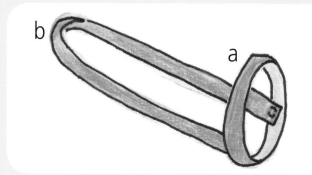

Figure K

Figure O

My Very Own Baby Doll

Do you remember your favorite baby doll? When I was young, my dolls were kids when I played house, students when I played school, and patients when I played doctor. This soft dolly is sure to give your child endless opportunities for play, and lots of fond memories.

EXPERIENCE LEVEL

DIMENSIONS

• 9" x 15" (23 cm x 38 cm)

MATERIALS

• Skin-color tricot (body, arms, legs): 18" x 35" (46 cm x 89 cm)
• Polyester fiberfill stuffing
• Plastic pellet stuffing (optional)
• Pink felt (lips): 1" x 1" (2.5 cm x 2.5 cm)
• Long pile faux fur (hair): 3" x 3" (7.5 cm x 7.5 cm)
• 1 bead (nose): about 1" (2.5 cm) diameter (large enough to make a nose-like bulge under the fabric)
• Skin-color and blue embroidery thread
• Skin-color thread
• Rouge for cheeks (optional)

TOOLS

• Chopstick
• Doll needle
• Fabric pen
• Iron
• Needle
• Pins
• Scissors
• Sewing machine
• Tailor's chalk

For a realistic feel, place plastic doll pellets inside a fabric pouch and add it to the bottom of the inner body and feet. These pellets add weight to the doll and make it feel a bit more substantial. If you can't find plastic doll pellets, substitute with kitty litter or sand.

You can use any color of fabric for the body that you like; select regular and embroidery thread that matches.

Getting Started

8 pattern pieces

• Copy the pattern pieces (page 113) and cut out.
• Trace the pattern pieces onto the fabric and cut out.

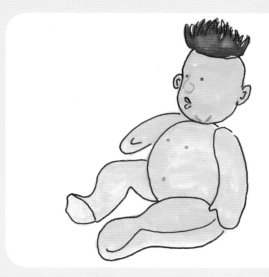

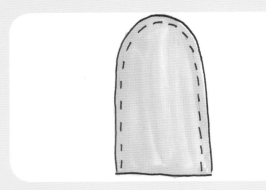

Figure A

Figure B

Figure C

Figure D

Instructions

Head

STEP 1

Pin both inner tube pieces together, right sides facing; sew all around, leaving the bottom open (Figure A).

STEP 2

Turn the tube right side out and firmly stuff the top 4" (10 cm). Tie a piece of embroidery thread immediately below the stuffed area of the tube to form the head (Figure B). (Holding the stuffing firmly in the head as you tie the thread can be a bit tricky, so ask someone to help you by holding the tube while you tie.)

STEP 3

Wrap a piece of pink embroidery thread horizontally around the middle of the head, and tie securely (Figure C). Tie a second piece of thread vertically around the middle of the head (Figure D). Tie both threads tight enough to make indentations in the head. These will help you arrange the features.

STEP 4

Draw the fabric creases you made in Step 2 to the back of the head, and try to smooth them out.

STEP 5

To make the nose, sew a bead in the center of the head, just below the horizontal thread (Figure E).

STEP 6

To prepare for the eyes, you'll make two indentations at the front of the head, just above the horizontally tied thread. To do this, knot a piece of pink embroidery thread, and sew into the head where one eye will be. Push the needle through the head and exit near the top, in a place that will be covered with hair (Figure F). Pull the thread to make an indentation on the face, and make a knot. Repeat for the second eye.

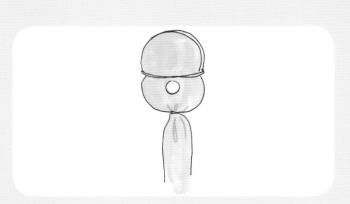

Figure E

STEP 7

Pin pairs of ear pieces together, right sides facing. Sew around each ear, leaving the straight edge open (Figure G).

STEP 8

Turn the ears right side out, insert a bit of stuffing into each ear, then slipstitch the opening to close. Using skin-color sewing thread, embroider a C in the middle of each ear with a running stitch (Figure H).

Body

STEP 9

Continue stuffing the inner tube until you reach the bottom. Pin the bottom and slipstitch to close (Figure I).

STEP 10

Pin both outer tube pieces together, right sides facing; sew all around, leaving the bottom open (Figure J).

STEP 11

Turn the outer tube right side out and pull over the inner tube (Figure K). The outer tube is just a bit bigger than the inner tube, and should fit snugly over it. Slipstitch the outer tube closed along the bottom.

Figure F

Figure G

Figure H

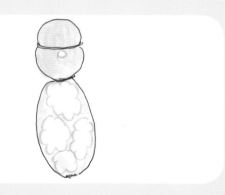

Figure I

Figure J

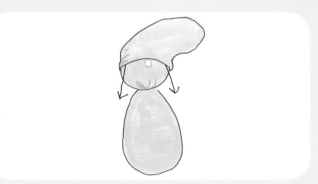

Figure K

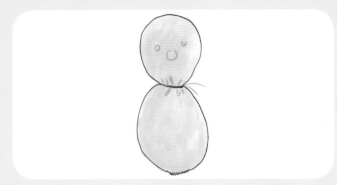

Figure L

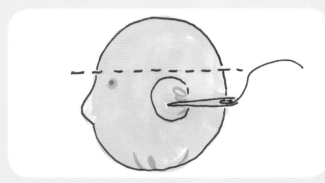

Figure M

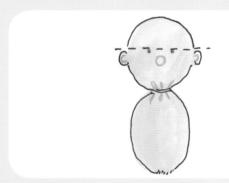

Figure N

Figure O

STEP 12

Tie a piece of pink embroidery thread tightly around the neck and draw the creases to the back of the head (Figure L).

STEP 13

With blue embroidery thread, make a French knot in each eye indentation.

STEP 14

Pin the ears onto the head, right sides facing, so that the top of each ear is even with the top of the eyes, and the rounded part of the ear faces forwards. Sew on the ear along the straight edge using slipstitch (Figure M); press the ear backward. The ear will now be attached to the side of the head, but the stitches will be concealed (Figure N).

STEP 15

Place the mouth piece below the nose. Embroider a horizontal line with backstitch across the middle of the mouth using sewing thread. Pin the hair piece on top of the head; sew all around with blanket stitch (Figure O).

STEP 16

Make 2 French knots for the baby's nipples. Pull the doll needle through the belly, pull and make a knot in the back. In this indentation, make one French knot for the baby's belly button (Figure P).

Figure P

Arms and legs

STEP 17

Pin pairs of arm pieces together, right sides facing. Sew all around, leaving an opening at the shoulder (Figure Q).

STEP 18

Turn arms right side out and stuff firmly; slipstitch the opening to close.

STEP 19

Pin pairs of leg pieces together, right sides facing. Sew all around, leaving openings at the bottom and the top (Figure R).

STEP 20

Pin a sole piece onto the bottom opening of each leg (Figure S); sew all around the sole.

STEP 21

Turn the legs right side out and stuff firmly with stuffing; slipstitch the opening to close.

STEP 22

With the doll needle, make a stitch in the inside top of one arm. Draw the needle through the body to the other side, then make a stitch in the inside top of the other arm. Push the needle back through the body and make a stitch in the first arm (Figures T and U).

STEP 23

Repeat this another two or three times, until both arms are securely affixed.

STEP 24

To finish, make a shank around the connection points of each arm and make a knot between the arm and body that can't be seen. Repeat this technique to attach the legs.

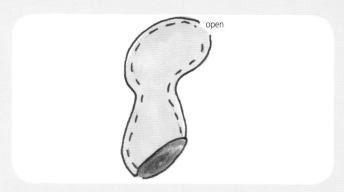

Figure R

Figure S

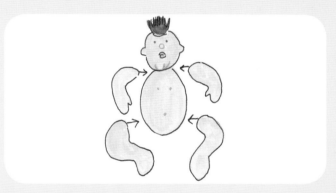

Figure T

Figure U

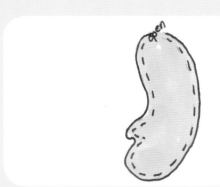

Figure Q

🐰 Baby Doll Clothes 🐰

These doll clothes replicate some of the favorite outfits that my girls wore growing up. The lacy white dress is a classic and the bunny feet pajamas were one thing they always asked to wear. Beautiful bonnets, bibs and carrot filled blankets will make your little girl's dolls the best dressed dolls on the block.

EXPERIENCE LEVEL

DIMENSIONS

• 24" x 16" (61 cm x 41 cm)

MATERIALS

Dress
• White cotton (dress, sleeves, skirt): 38" x 20" (97 cm x 51 cm)
• Lace (neck, arms): 20" (51 cm)
• Elastic (sleeves): ⅛" (0.3 cm) thick, 16" (40 cm)
• Velcro®: 2 pieces, each 1½" x 1½" (4 cm x 4 cm)
• Matching thread

Pajamas
• White tricot (pajamas): 15" x 25" (38 cm x 64 cm)
• Velcro®: 1 piece, 4" x 1" (10 cm x 2.5 cm)
• White felt (bunny face, bunny ears): 4" x 4" (10 cm x 10 cm)
• Orange felt (carrot appliqué): 1½" x 1" (4 cm x 2.5 cm)
• Pink felt (inside of bunny ears): 2" x 2" (5 cm x 5 cm)
• Orange, white, pink and green embroidery thread
• Matching thread

Bib
• Cotton: 5" x 5" (13 cm x 13 cm)
• Bias tape, ½" (1.2 cm), (for tying): 10" (25 cm)
• Matching thread

Diaper
• White fleece: 9" x 9" (23 cm x 23 cm)
• Velcro®: 2 pieces, each 1" x 1" (2.5 cm x 2.5 cm)
• Matching thread

Blanket
• Flannel: 16" x 25" (41 cm x 64 cm)
• Orange and green embroidery thread

Bonnet
• Cotton: 16" x 6" (41 cm x 15 cm)
• Elastic: ⅛" thick, 2½" (6 cm)
• Bias tape, ¼" (0.6 mm), (for tying): 22" (56 cm)
• Matching thread

TOOLS

• Embroidery needle
• Fabric pen
• Iron
• Needle
• Pins
• Scissors
• Sewing machine
• Tailor's chalk

Doll clothes are sewn a little differently than real clothes because of their small size.

I cut this doll dress and bonnet from antique fabric made with pre-sewn pleats and lace. If you use antique fabric, make sure to lay the pattern on it so that the lace or special sewing is along the bottom of the skirt or the end of the bonnet brim. The instructions below show the dress and bonnet without pre-sewn laced fabric.

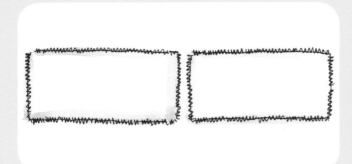

Figure A

Figure B

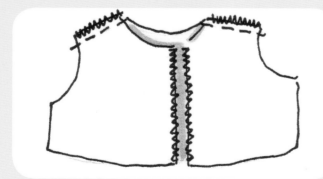

Figure C

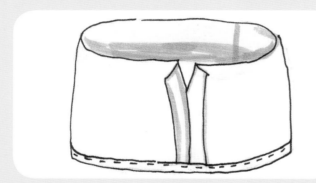

Figure D

Getting Started

14 pattern pieces

- Copy the pattern pieces (pages 114–116) and cut out.
- Trace the pattern pieces onto the fabric and cut.

Instructions

Dress

STEP 1

Over-lock or zigzag the edges of the skirt pieces (Figure A).

STEP 2

Pin the skirt pieces together, right sides facing, and sew both vertical seams to form a tube shape. On one seam, start sewing 1" (2.5 cm) down from the top (this seam becomes part of the back opening of the dress) (Figure B). Hem the bottom of the skirt (Figure C).

STEP 3

Gather the top of the skirt.

STEP 4

Pin the back and front bodice pieces together, right sides facing; sew together at the shoulders. Over-lock or zigzag the seams at the shoulders and the back opening (Figure D). Hem the back opening.

STEP 5

Over-lock the edges of the sleeve pieces; hem sleeve edge (see pattern). Sew lace along the edge of each sleeve seam allowance (Figure E).

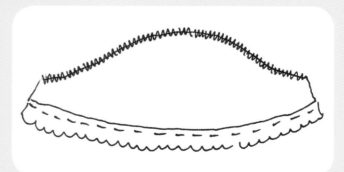

Figure E

STEP 6

Cut the elastic into two even pieces and sew one piece along the edge of each sleeve, on the wrong side, over the hem. Pull on the elastic as you sew, so that the sleeve gathers as you sew (Figure F).

STEP 7

Gather the top of each sleeve (Figure G).

STEP 8

Line up the gathered part of the sleeves with the arm holes in the bodice, right sides facing; pin. Sew around each sleeve (Figure H).

STEP 9

Over-lock or zigzag around the neck; hem (Figure I). Sew lace around the neck (Figure J).

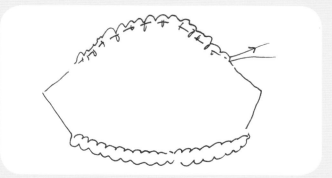

Figure G

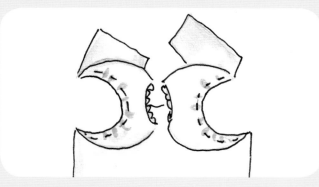

Figure H

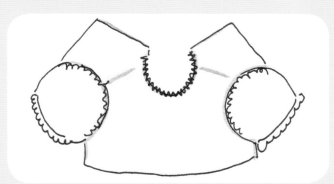

Figure I

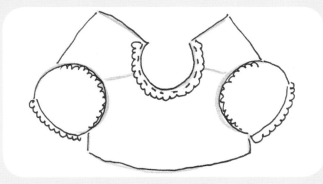

Figure J

Figure F

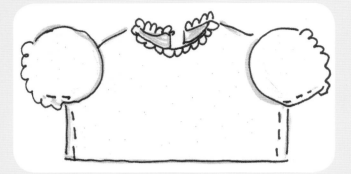

Figure K

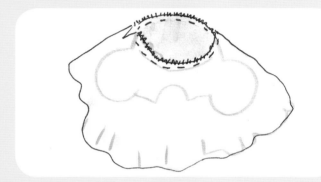

Figure L

Figure M

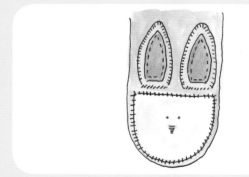

Figure N

STEP 10

Pin the bodice front to the bodice back pieces, right sides together, matching sleeve edges. Sew side and underarm seams (Figure K). Turn right side out, press.

STEP 11

Put bodice inside the skirt, right sides facing. Line up the opening of the bodice with the small opening in the skirt.

STEP 12

Pin the bodice and skirt together at the waist; sew all around. Overlock or zigzag the seam (Figure L).

STEP 13

Sew corresponding sides of Velcro® onto the top and bottom of dress opening (see pattern) (Figure M).

Pajamas

STEP 14

Pin one bunny face piece on each foot of the pajama front piece, leaving room to sew seam; embroider all around with blanket stitch.

STEP 15

Pin the inside ear pieces onto the outside ear pieces; embroider all around with blanket stitch.

STEP 16

Pin two bunny ears onto the top of each bunny face; slipstitch the bottom edge of the ears onto the bunny face. Embroider two eyes with French knots and a nose with a satin stitch on each bunny face (Figure N).

STEP 17

Pin the carrot piece to the right upper corner of the front pajama piece. Embroider around the carrot with blanket stitch. Embroider carrot leaves with chain stitch (Figure O).

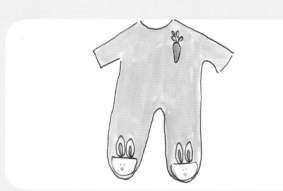

Figure O

STEP 18

Sew front shoulder seams using over-lock or zigzag stitch. Over-lock or zigzag the back opening, around the neck and the edges of the sleeves. Hem the back opening and around the neck and sleeves (Figure P).

STEP 19

Flip the front piece over and pin the left and right back pieces together at the back seam, right sides facing; sew the back seam to the notch.

STEP 20

Sew corresponding sides of Velcro® onto each side of the back opening (Figure Q).

STEP 21

Pin the pajama front and back together, right sides facing, matching up the sleeve and leg pieces.

STEP 22

Start at the bottom inner edge of one sleeve, and sew along the inner sleeve, down the side, around both feet, and up to the inner bottom edge of the other sleeve. Be careful to not catch the bunny appliqué in the seam around the feet (Figure R). Over-lock or zigzag the seam turn right side out, press.

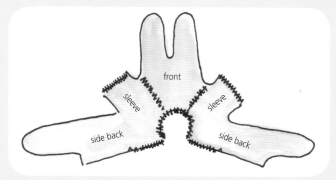

Figure P

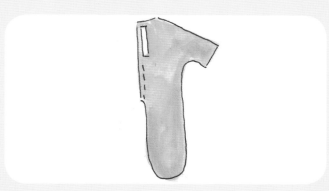

Figure Q

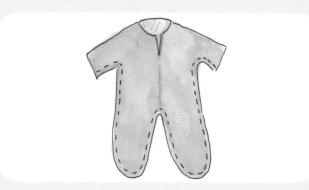

Figure R

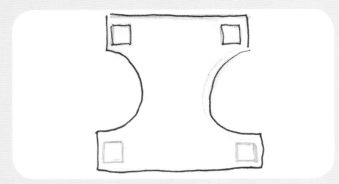

Figure S

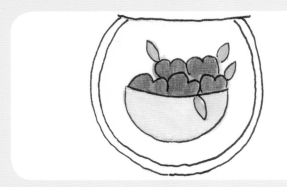

Figure T

Figure U

Diaper

STEP 23

Sew corresponding sides of Velcro® onto the four corners of the diaper (see pattern) (Figure S).

Bib

STEP 24

Sew bias tape around the round part of the bib (Figure T).

STEP 25

Sew bias tape around the neck of the bib, leaving an extra 6" (15 cm) on each side for tying (Figure U); press.

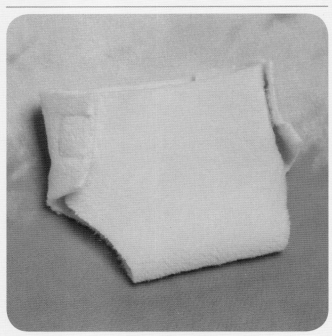

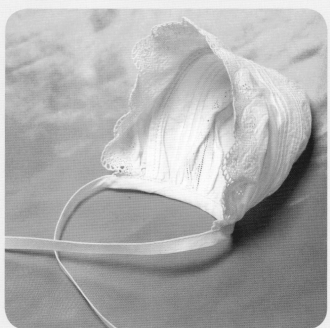

Bonnet

STEP 26

Pin the brim piece to the back piece, right sides facing (Figure V); sew back seam. Over-lock or zigzag the seam (Figure W).

STEP 27

Gather the edges until bonnet fits snuggly around the doll's head (Figure X).

STEP 28

Sew bias tape around the neck, leaving an extra 6" (15 cm) extra on each side for tying (Figure Y); press.

Blanket

STEP 29

Embroider around blanket piece with blanket stitch.

STEP 30

Embroider carrot shapes in the opposite corners (see pattern) with backstitch. Embroider carrot leaves with chain stitch.

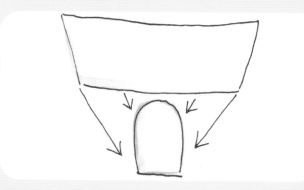

Figure V

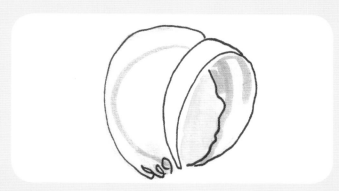

Figure W

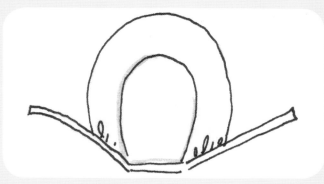

Figure X

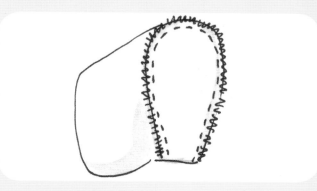

Figure Y

Pop Star Microphone

For anyone who loves to perform, this soft microphone is sure to be a #1 hit. It can be used for an a cappella performance or accompanied by some background music. It can also be used for storytelling, comedy routines and any other activities that merit higher volume than usual!

EXPERIENCE LEVEL

DIMENSIONS

• 4" x 12" (10 cm x 30 cm)

MATERIALS

• Shiny silver fabric (handle, bottom): 13" x 14" (33 cm x 36 cm)
• Sparkly blue fabric (microphone head): 7" x 14" (18 cm x 36 cm)
• Iron-on fabric stabilizer (handle and head): 13" x 19" (33 cm x 48 cm)
• Decorative trim: 10" (25 cm)
• Polyester fiberfill stuffing
• Gray thread

TOOLS

• Fabric pen
• Iron
• Needle
• Pins
• Scissors
• Sewing machine

Opposite: Use blue, pink or any other color of sparkly fabric you like for the top of the microphone.

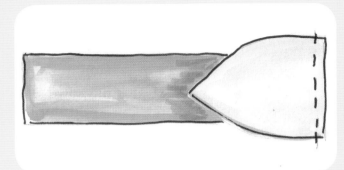

Figure A

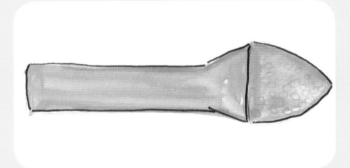

Figure B

Getting Started

3 pattern pieces

- Copy the pattern pieces (page 117) and cut out.
- Iron fabric stabilizer onto the back of the shiny and sparkly fabrics.
- Trace microphone pattern pieces onto fabric and cut out.

Instructions

STEP 1

To make one side of the microphone, pin one top piece onto one handle piece, straight edges aligned and right sides facing. Sew across the straight edge (Figure A).

STEP 2

Fold up the microphone top; press (Figure B).

STEP 3

Repeat steps 1 and 2 to make the other three microphone sides.

STEP 4

Pin two microphone sides together, right sides facing. Sew together along one side, from top to bottom (Figure C).

STEP 5

Sew the last side, leaving an opening in the last side seam, to make a tube shape with a closed top and open bottom.

STEP 6

Pin the bottom piece onto the bottom of the microphone, right sides facing; sew together all around (Figures D and E).

STEP 7

Turn the microphone right side out. Stuff firmly with stuffing; slipstitch the opening to close.

STEP 8

Pin decorative trim around the top seam of the microphone; hand sew (Figure F).

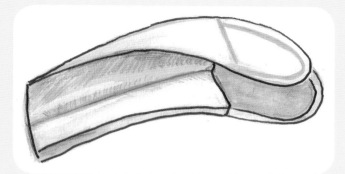

Figure C

Figure D

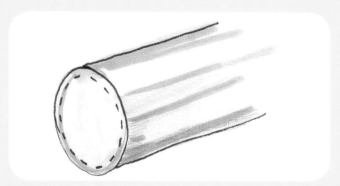

Figure E

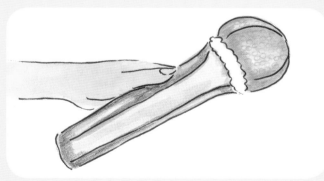

Figure F

My Favorite Mermaid

This little doll will accompany your child on every imaginary underwater adventure, and help create a watery wonderland of sea creature friends, underwater caves and sunken treasures.

EXPERIENCE LEVEL

DIMENSIONS

- 19½" x11" (50 cm x 28 cm)

MATERIALS

- Skin-color tricot (upper body): 12" x 15" (30 cm x 38 cm)
- Stretchy sequined fabric (lower body): 9" x 12" (23 cm x 30 cm)
- Green velvet (fin): 10" x 13" (25 cm x 33 cm)
- Foam, ⅛"–¹⁄₁₆" (3 mm–1.5 mm) thick (fin) 5" x 13" (13 cm x 33 cm)
- Red felt (mouth): 1" x 1" (2.5 cm x 2.5 cm)
- 1 bead (nose): ¹⁄₁₆" (2 mm)
- Polyester fiberfill stuffing
- Orange yarn (hair)
- Orange felt (wig): 3" x 4" (7.5 cm x 10 cm)
- White felt (bra): 2" x 4" (5 cm x 10 cm)
- Green ribbon (fin): 15" (38 cm)
- Decorative trim (waist): 7" (18 cm)
- Black and skin-color embroidery thread
- Orange, red, green and skin-color thread
- Glitter glue (bra, optional)

TOOLS

- Chopstick
- Doll needle
- Embroidery needle
- Fabric glue
- Fabric pen
- Iron
- Needle
- Paint brush
- Pins
- Scissors
- Sewing machine
- Tailor's chalk

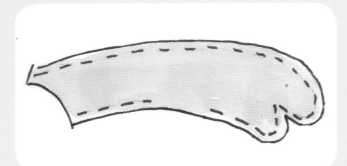

Figure A

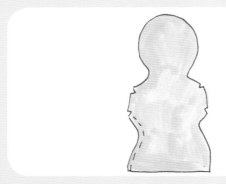

Figure B

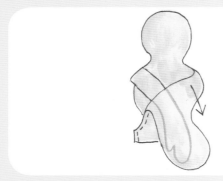

Figure C

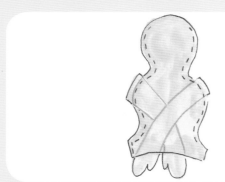

Figure D

Getting Started

8 pattern pieces

• Copy the pattern pieces (page 118) and cut out
• Trace the pattern pieces onto the fabric and cut out.

Instructions

Arms and upper body

STEP 1

Pin two arm pieces together, right sides facing; sew all around, leaving openings on the underside and at the inside end for sewing into the body (Figure A). Repeat with the other two arm pieces. Turn right side out; press.

STEP 2

Pin the front and back upper body pieces together, right sides facing. Starting at the bottom, sew along one side until the first notch (see pattern) (Figure B).

STEP 3

Fold open the top of the upper body and insert one arm, inwards and thumb down (Figure C).

STEP 4

Fold back the upper body top and continue sewing until the top of the head. Leave an opening along the top (for stuffing the head) then sew until the next notch (see pattern).

STEP 5

Fold open the bottom of the upper body and insert the other arm, inwards and thumb down. Fold back the upper body bottom and continue sewing until the bottom. Leave the bottom open (Figure D).

Lower body and fin

STEP 6

Pin the bottom flap of one lower body piece to one fin piece, right sides out. Sew together along the V (Figure E). Repeat with the other lower body piece and fin piece.

STEP 7

For a clean finish, pin ribbon over the seams of the V on the front and back; sew down on both sides of each ribbon piece (Figure F).

STEP 8

Pin both lower body with fin pieces together, right sides facing. Pin the fin foam piece onto the outside of one side of each fin. Sew around the lower body and the fin, stopping about 2 " (5 cm) before the top (waist) (Figure G).

STEP 9

Insert upper body head first into lower body, right sides facing; sew around the waist (Figure H).

STEP 10

Sew up 1 " (2.5 cm) more of the lower body. Turn right side out and insert stuffing; slipstitch the opening to close.

STEP 11

Stuff the arms; slipstitch the openings to close.

STEP 12

With skin-color embroidery thread, push the doll needle into the belly, and sew through to the other side, close to the waist (to hide the stitch) (Figure I). Pull and knot the thread to make a belly button.

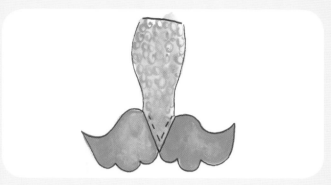

Figure F

Figure G

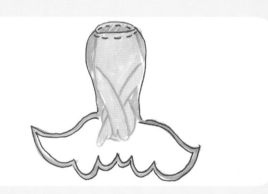

Figure H

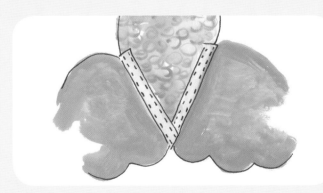

Figure E

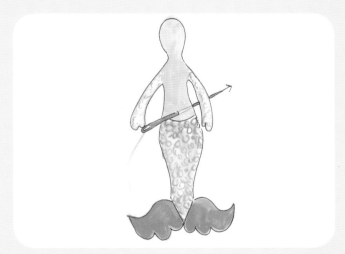

Figure I

73

Figure J

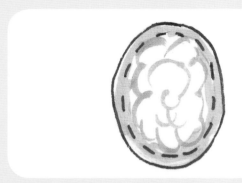

Figure K

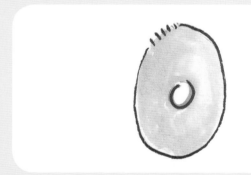

Figure L

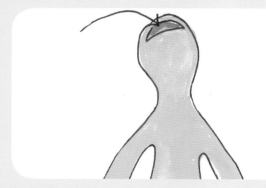

Figure M

STEP 13

Pin decorative trim around the waist; hand sew (Figure J).

Face

STEP 14

Pin the head pillow pieces together, right sides facing. Sew all around, leaving a small opening. Turn right side out and stuff firmly; slipstitch the opening to close (Figure K).

STEP 15

Sew on a small bead in the middle front of the head for the nose (Figure L).

STEP 16

Insert the head pillow into the slit in the head (Figure M) and push it to the front. Fill the back of the head with stuffing (Figure N); slipstitch the opening to close.

STEP 17

Embroider two French knots for the eyes. Pin on the mouth piece and embroider a horizontal line with backstitch (Figure O).

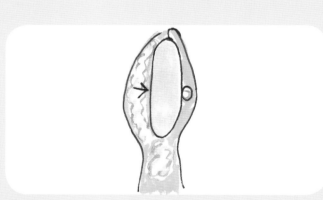

Figure N

Figure O

Wig

STEP 18

Cut several 15" (38 cm) strands of yarn. Lay the strands lengthwise on the wig piece, so that the yarn ends are aligned with one rounded edge; sew down (Figure P).

STEP 19

Cut several 30" (76 cm) strands of yarn. Lay these strands horizontally across the wig piece, so that they hang evenly on either side; sew down (Figure Q).

STEP 20

Glue the wig piece onto the head, so that it covers the slit that was used for stuffing; slipstitch all around the wig.

Shell bra

STEP 21

Accordion fold both bra pieces; hand sew the folds together at the bottom to make shell shapes (Figure R). Paint the shells with glitter glue (optional) and hand sew onto the mermaid's chest (Figure S).

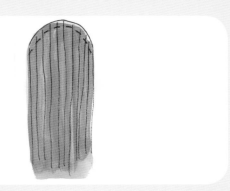

Figure P

Figure Q

Figure R

Figure S

Handy Dandy Tool Belt and Tools

Does your child know the difference between a claw hammer, a ball-peen hammer and a sledge hammer? If not, maybe it's time they learn! Start your kids off in Tools 101 with this Handy Dandy Tool Belt. Fill it with Tools (pages 81-83) and they'll be ready to fix anything!

EXPERIENCE LEVEL

Belt

Tools

DIMENSIONS

- Belt: 31" x 7" (79 cm x 18 cm)
- Wrench: 7" x 1½" (18 cm x 4 cm)
- Saw: 9" x 2½" (23 cm x 6 cm)
- Hammer: 8" x 5" (20 cm x 13 cm)
- Screwdriver: 7" x 1½" (18 cm x 4 cm)

MATERIALS

- Brown corduroy, denim or faux suede (belt, pouch, loop): 19" x 32" (48 cm x 81 cm)
- Brown thread
- Velcro®: 1 piece, 3" x 1" (8 cm x 2.5 cm)
- Shiny silver fabric (metal part of tools): 10" x 22" (25 cm x 56 cm)
- Red denim (hammer handle): 6" x 9" (15 cm x 23 cm)
- Yellow denim (screwdriver handle): 6" x 10" (15 cm x 25 cm)
- Blue denim (saw handle): 6" x 6" (15 cm x 15 cm)
- Iron-on fabric stabilizer, medium (tools): 20" x 23" (51 cm x 58 cm)
- Foam, ⅛"–1/16" (3 mm–1.5 mm) thick (saw blade): 6" x 8" (15 cm x 20 cm)
- Polyester fiberfill stuffing
- Thin craft plastic (saw reinforcement): 3½" x 7" (9 cm x 18 cm)

TOOLS

- Fabric pen
- Iron
- Pins
- Scissors
- Sewing machine
- Tailor's chalk

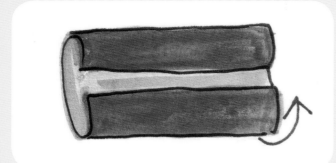

Figure A

Figure B

Figure C

Figure D

Getting Started

11 pattern pieces (Belt: 3 pieces; Wrench: 1 piece; Hammer: 3 pieces; Saw: 3 pieces; Screwdriver: 2 pieces)

• Copy the pattern pieces (pages 119–120) and cut out.

• Iron fabric stabilizer onto all the fabric you'll use to make the tools.

• Trace the pattern pieces onto the fabric and cut out.

Instructions

Side loops

STEP 1

Fold the long sides of one side loop piece toward the center (Figure A); press.

STEP 2

Fold the loop piece in half again, encasing the raw edges (Figure B); press.

STEP 3

Sew along both long sides, close to the edge (Figure C).

STEP 4

Fold the loop piece in half widthwise; press. Sew the short ends together to form a loop (Figure D). Repeat with the other side loop piece.

Pouches

STEP 5

Make a ¼" (0.6 cm) fold along one short side of one pouch piece (see pattern); pin. Sew along fold (Figure E); press.

Figure E

STEP 6

Pin both loops on the inside of one side of one pouch piece (see pattern). Fold the pouch up, right sides together, until the notch (Figure F).

STEP 7

Sew along both sides of the pouch, securing the loops (Figure G).

STEP 8

Make a ⅜" (1 cm) cut on both sides of the pouch, where the top of the pouch lines up with the notch (Figure H).

STEP 9

Turn the pouch over, so that the wrong side faces up. Fold over the two small flaps (made from the cut at the top of the belt loop); press, sew (Figure I).

STEP 10

Fold the top of the fabric down to the top of the pouch; pin. This folded area is the loop that slides onto the belt. Sew down the edge of the folded fabric (Figure J); turn the pouch right side out.

Figure F

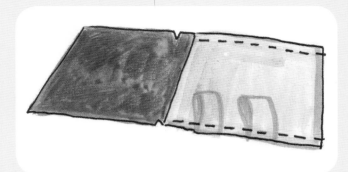

Figure G

Figure H

Figure I

Figure J

Figure K

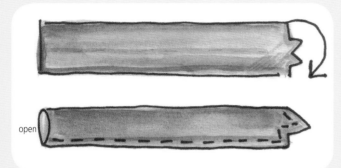

Figure L

Figure M

Figure N

STEP 11

Stitch down the center of the pouch, dividing it into two smaller pockets (Figure K).

STEP 12

Repeat steps above to make second pouch without the loops.

Belt

STEP 13

Fold the belt piece in half lengthwise, right sides together; press. Sew along the long side and pointed end (Figure L). Turn right side out; press.

STEP 14

Tuck the raw edges in to the open end of the belt, and pin corresponding sides of Velcro® onto each end of the belt. Sew on Velcro®, closing the open end of the belt at the same time (Figure M).

STEP 15

Slide the belt through the loop at the top of each pouch (Figure N).

Wrench

STEP 16

Pin both wrench pieces together, right sides facing. Sew around the shape, leaving an opening along the straight edge of the handle (Figure O).

STEP 17

Turn the wrench right side out and stuff firmly with stuffing. Slipstitch the opening to close; press.

Hammer

STEP 18

Pin one hammer head piece to one hammer handle piece, right sides facing. Sew together (Figure P); press open. Repeat with the other hammer head and handle pieces.

STEP 19

Pin the front and back of the hammer together, right sides facing. Sew around the shape, leaving an opening along the straight edge of the head and on one side of the handle (Figure Q).

STEP 20

With wrong sides out, pin the hammer head face piece into the open part of the hammer head, right sides facing (Figure R); sew.

STEP 21

Turn the hammer right side out and stuff firmly with stuffing. Slipstitch the opening to close.

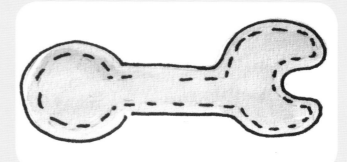

Figure O

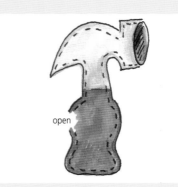

Figure P

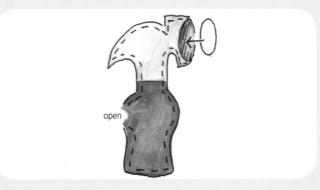

Figure Q

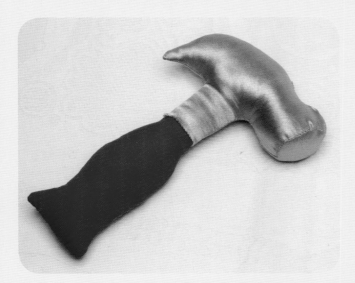

Figure R

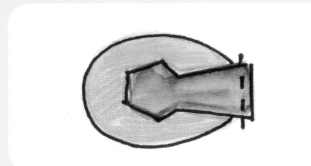

Figure S

Figure T

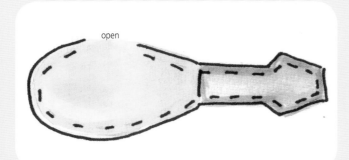

open

Figure U

Screwdriver

STEP 22

Pin one screwdriver head piece to one screwdriver handle piece, right sides facing. Sew together (Figure S); press open (Figure T). Repeat with the other head and handle pieces.

STEP 23

Pin the front and back of the screwdriver together, right sides facing. Sew around the shape, leaving an opening along one side of the handle (Figure U).

STEP 24

Turn the screwdriver right side out and stuff firmly with stuffing. Slipstitch the opening to close; press.

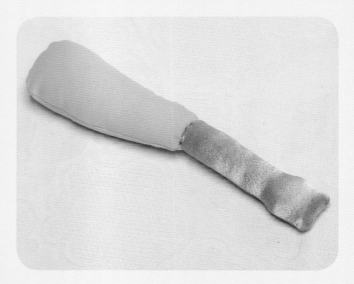

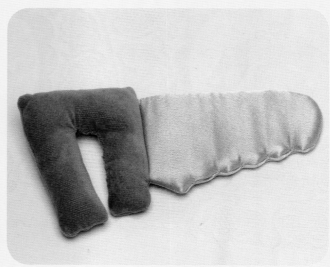

Saw

STEP 25

Pin each foam blade piece to the corresponding fabric blade piece. Sew around each shape, close to the edge.

STEP 26

Pin the front blade to one saw handle piece, right sides facing. Sew together (Figure V); press open (Figure W).

STEP 27

Pin the back blade piece to the front blade piece. Pin the back handle piece to the front handle piece (Figure X). Note that unlike the front of the saw, the back is not sewn together between the blade and the handle.

STEP 28

Sew all around the shape, leaving an opening between the back blade and handle piece (Figure Y). Turn right side out.

STEP 29

Slide the plastic inner saw piece into the blade through the opening between the back blade and handle. Stuff the handle firmly with stuffing (Figure Z). Slipstitch the opening to close.

Figure W

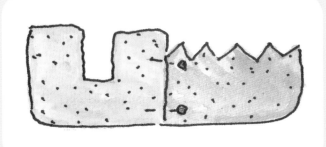

Figure X

Figure Y

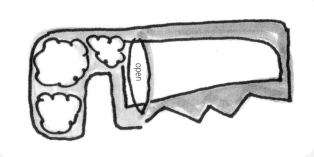

Figure Z

Figure V

Plundering Pirate Ship

Children will invent countless adventures with this little pirate ship. Just give it a worthy name, hoist the sails up high, and venture out into the deep blue sea! Make sure they watch out for the giant Kraken (page 25), violent storms and other plundering pirates!

EXPERIENCE LEVEL

DIMENSIONS

• 20" x 21" (51 cm x 53 cm)

MATERIALS

• White felt (sails, skull appliqué): 22" x 32" (56 cm x 81 cm)
• Black felt (flag): 4" x 8" (10 cm x 20 cm)
• Red fabric (ship trim): 10" x 24" (25 cm x 61 cm)
• Brown denim or faux suede (outer ship): 27" x 24" (69 cm x 61 cm)
• Yellow denim (inner ship): 27" x 24" (69 cm x 61 cm)
• Foam, ¼" (0.6 cm) thick (inner ship layer): 36" x 41" (92 cm x 104 cm)
• Foam, about ⅜" (1 cm) thick (mast support): 9" x 15" (23 cm x 38 cm)
• One-sided iron-on fabric stabilizer, heavy (outer ship, inner ship, ship trim): 36" x 41" (92 cm x 104 cm)
• Double-sided iron-on fabric stabilizer (skull appliqué): 3" x 4" (7.5 cm x 10 cm)
• Dowel rod: ¼" (0.6 cm) diameter x 40" (102 cm)
• Yellow bias tape, ½" (1.2 cm) thick, (top and bottom ship edge (inner and outer), dowel rods): 155" (394 cm)
• Gold trim (optional, outside of ship): 116" (295 cm)
• Red, brown, yellow and white thread
• Brown marker
• Fabric glue

TOOLS

• Craft saw (to cut dowel rods)
• Doll needle
• Fabric glue
• Fabric pen
• Iron
• Needle
• Pins
• Pliers
• Safety pin
• Scissors
• Sewing machine
• Tailor's chalk
• Thimble
• Triangle ruler

Getting Started

13 pattern pieces

• Copy the pattern pieces (pages 121–123) and cut out.
• Iron one-sided fabric stabilizer onto the back of the brown, yellow and red fabric.
• Iron double-sided fabric stabilizer onto the back of a piece of white felt that is large enough to cut out white skull appliqué piece.
• Cut the dowel rod into two pieces, each 20" (51 cm) long.
• Trace the pieces onto the fabric and cut out.

Opposite: Fear the Kraken! (pages 25-27), Plundering Pirate Ship (pages 85-89), Ahoy! It's a Pirate Hat (pages 31-32) and Pirate Ship Dolls and Treasure Chest (pages 91-101)

Figure A

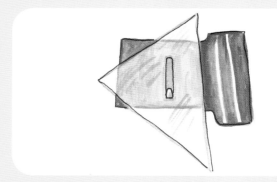

Figure B

Figure C

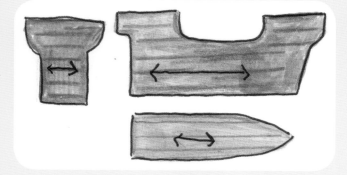

Figure D

Instructions

Sails and flag

STEP 1

Pin front and back small sail pieces right sides together. Sew all around, leaving an opening in the bottom. Turn right side out; press. Slipstitch the opening to close. Repeat with other small sail pieces and large sail pieces to make all four sails (Figure A).

STEP 2

Iron the appliqué onto the center of the front flag piece (Figure B).

STEP 3

Pin the front and back flag pieces together, right sides facing. Sew around, leaving an opening on one side. Turn right side out; press. Slipstitch the opening to close.

Ship

STEP 4

Pin the outer and inner ship foam pieces onto the wrong side of their corresponding fabric pieces. Sew around each shape close to the edge.

STEP 5

To make lines that give the impression of wood, mark horizontal sewing lines at 1" (2.5 cm) intervals onto the side, back and bottom inner and outer ship pieces. Start marking the lines 1" (2.5 cm) from the top of each piece. Use the triangle ruler to draw straight lines across the ship pieces. Mark similar lines across the length of the bottom inner and outer ship pieces (Figures C and D).

STEP 6

Use brown thread to sew along the lines on the outer pieces. Use yellow thread to sew along the lines on the inner pieces.

STEP 7

Place the side trim pieces on the outer side pieces (see pattern); pin. Pin the U shape first, and make sure the front of the trim piece is at the front of the side piece (Figure E). Pin the back trim piece to the outer ship back piece (see pattern).

STEP 8

With red thread, sew all around each trim piece; zigzag the bottom edge of the trim.

STEP 9

Sew bias tape along the top edges of the outer ship, encasing the raw edges.

STEP 10

Pin the outer ship pieces together, right sides facing, with the front of the side pieces connected to each other, and the back of the side pieces connected to the end piece. Pin the bottom piece to the sides and end piece, right sides facing (Figure F).

> Sewing the corners of the ship can be difficult. Instead of starting to sew in a corner, start sewing at the center of a side, and sew into the corner.

STEP 11

Make sure the red trim is lined up all around the ship, so that it forms a single smooth line (Figure G).

STEP 12

Sew the sides, end and bottom pieces together. The pieces are thick so pull them slowly through the sewing machine. Trim the corners (Figure H). Turn the outer ship right side out; press.

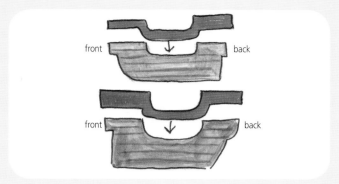

Figure E

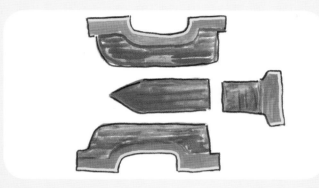

Figure F

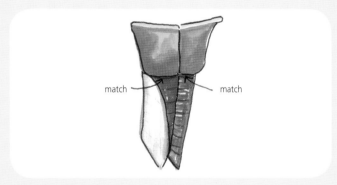

Figure G

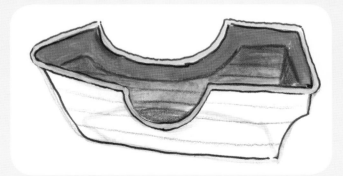

Figure H

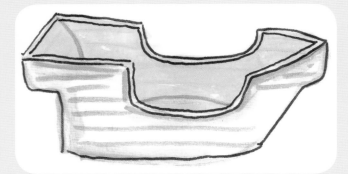

Figure I

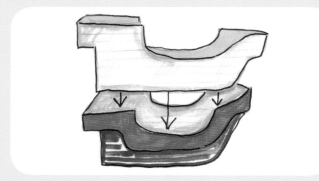

Figure J

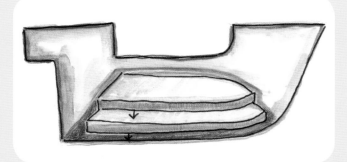

Figure K

Figure L

STEP 13

Sew bias tape along the top edges of the inner ship pieces, encasing the raw edges. Assemble the inner ship pieces as you did the outer ship pieces to make the inner ship (Figure I).

STEP 14

Glue the foam mast support pieces into the bottom of the outside ship (Figure J).

STEP 15

Place the inner ship into the outer ship, pushing the corners in firmly; pin all around (Figure K).

STEP 16

Slipstitch the inner and outer ship together along the top edge (Figure L).

STEP 17

With yellow thread and a doll needle, make small stitches all over the ship to hold the outer and inner ship closer together. Make the stitches small enough so that they can't be seen. If yellow stitches are visible on the outside of the ship, color them with a brown marker.

> Use pliers to pull the needle through the ship and a thimble to push it.

STEP 18

Pin gold trim around the top edge of the ship and the bottom of the red trim (optional); glue or hand sew. (The gold trim gives the ship a more pirate-like feel and covers the stitches for a cleaner look.)

Masts

STEP 19

Using scissors, carefully cut two shallow holes through the inner ship bottom and foam mast support (see pattern). Do not cut all the way through the outer bottom layer (Figure M).

STEP 20

Put glue into the holes and insert one dowel rod into each hole. Let the glue dry.

STEP 21

Cut two 20" (50 cm) pieces of bias tape and iron them flat. Fold both pieces in half lengthwise and sew near the edge, along the open side and one end. Turn right side out and pull over the dowel rods (Figure N). Slipstitch the end of the bias tape tube to the inner bottom of the ship (Figure O).

STEP 22

Pin the Jolly Roger flag onto the top of the front mast so that it faces the front of the ship. Pin one small white sail to the top of each mast, so that the top of the sail is about 3½" (9 cm) below the top of the mast. Orient the sails so that they face forwards and are centered on the mast.

STEP 23

Pin one large sail onto each mast, about 8¼" (21 cm) below the top of the mast. Orient the sails so that they face forwards and are centered on the mast (Figures P and Q).

STEP 24

Sew the sails onto the mast covers at the center top and bottom of each sail. Push the bottom of each sail up a little bit so that the sail puffs out slightly.

Figure N

Figure O

Figure P

Figure Q

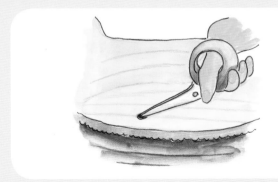

Figure M

Pirate Ship Dolls and Treasure Chest

Yo ho ho! Kids love these pirate characters, and I have a few guesses why. Is it because they don't have to take a bath? Because they're not lily-livered? Because they sail in grand ships, battle fierce creatures, carry sharp swords, and hunt for booty? Whatever the reason, these swashbuckling characters will help your wee landlubbers have a jolly good time!

EXPERIENCE LEVEL

DIMENSIONS

- Pirate Captain: 6" x 3" (15 cm x 8 cm)
- Mate: 6" x 3" (15 cm x 8 cm)
- Wench: 6" x 2" (15 cm x 5 cm)
- Mermaid: 3½" x 5½" (9 cm x 14 cm)
- Treasure Chest: 1½" x 2" x 2" (4 cm x 5 cm x 5 cm)

Each doll is made in the same basic way:
by placing felt pieces onto the felt body base,
sewing around each piece with matching thread,
adding appendages or 3-D parts, gluing/sewing
on the back body piece for extra support; covering
the stitching from the front. Follow the order of
application specified for each doll.

All of these pieces are sewn entirely by hand.
I recommend having several needles threaded with
matching thread so that they are ready to use.

MATERIALS

- Listed separately for each element

TOOLS

- Tools
- Fabric pen
- Iron
- Needle
- Small paintbrush
- Small scissors
- Tailor's chalk
- Thimble

Felt is usually sold by the yard, or in 8½" x 11"
(21 cm x 28 cm) pieces. One 8½" x 11" piece
(21 cm x 28 cm) of felt in each listed color will be
enough to make all the projects.

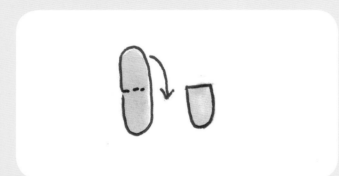

Captain

MATERIALS

- Felt:
  - Gray (hook): 2" x 2" (5 cm x 5 cm)
  - Red (jacket, sleeves, bandana): 3½" x 3½" (9 cm x 9 cm)
  - Black (body base front/back, hat, beard): 4" x 7" (10 cm x 18 cm)
  - Yellow ochre (peg leg): 1" x 2" (2.5 cm x 5 cm)
  - White (sleeve ruffles, jabot): 2½" x 5" (6 cm x 13 cm)
  - Dark brown (boot): 2" x 2½" (5 cm x 6 cm)
  - Light brown (boot cuff): 1½" x 1½" (4 cm x 4 cm)
  - Skin-color (face, nose, hand): 2" x 2" (5 cm x 5 cm)
- Black iron-on fabric stabilizer: 4" x 7" (10 cm x 18 cm)
- White, black, red, gray, brown and yellow ochre thread
- Gold embroidery thread
- White acrylic paint
- Fabric glue
- Polyester fiberfill stuffing (sleeves)

Getting Started

15 pattern pieces

- Copy the pattern pieces (page124) and cut out.
- Iron fabric stabilizer onto the back of all the fabric.
- Trace the pieces onto the fabric and cut out.

Instructions

Hand

STEP 1

Fold the hand piece in half; stitch around the shape (Figure A).

Figure A

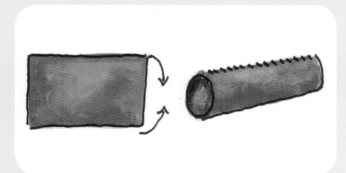

Sleeves

STEP 2

Roll each sleeve piece to form a tube and slipstitch along seam (Figure B). Fill with stuffing.

STEP 3

Gather each sleeve ruffle piece; press. Slipstitch the ruffles to secure.

Figure B

STEP 4

Put a ruffle into one end of each sleeve (Figure C).

STEP 5

Stitch the hand piece into one sleeve and the hook piece into the other sleeve; close the sleeve ends (Figure D).

STEP 6

Using red thread, stitch each sleeve onto the jacket piece, at the shoulder.

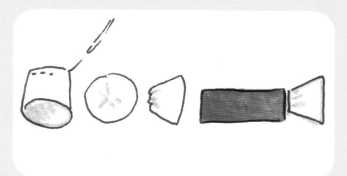

Figure C

Jabot

STEP 7

Accordion fold the jabot piece.

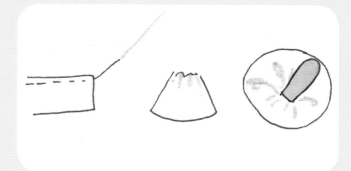

Figure D

Nose

STEP 8

Roll the nose piece into a tube then fold it in half horizontally; stitch to close.

Order of Application

STEP 9

Apply a dot of glue to the wrong side of the small pieces and affix in the following order: body base front, face, bandana, nose, jacket (with attached arms), jabot, beard, peg leg, boot, boot cuff, hat.

STEP 10

Stitch around each piece with matching thread. Glue the body base back onto the front body, wrong sides facing. Cut out the space between the peg leg and the boot; stitch around the entire body shape with matching thread.

Embellishments

STEP 11

Embroider eyes, a mouth and dots on the bandana. Using 1 strand of gold embroidery thread, embroider gold trim on the jacket with backstitch and French knots.

STEP 12

Paint a skull and crossbones on the hat using a very small paintbrush and white acrylic paint.

First Mate

MATERIALS

- Felt:
  - Brown (body base): 3½" x 5½" (9 cm x 14 cm)
  - Yellow ochre (pants): 2" x 3" (5 cm x 8 cm)
  - Red (sash-3parts, bandana): 3" x 3" (8 cm x 8 cm)
  - White (sleeves, shirt center, jabot): 4" x 5" (10 cm x 13 cm)
  - Black (eye patch): 1" x 1" (2.5 cm x 2.5 cm)
  - Skin-color (face, hands, feet): 2" x 4" (5 cm x 10 cm)
- Black iron-on fabric stabilizer: 3½" x 5½" (9 cm x 14 cm)
- Skin-color red, brown, yellow ochre, white and black thread
- Gold embroidery thread
- Fabric glue
- Poly fiberfill stuffing for sleeves

Getting Started

13 pattern pieces

- Copy the pattern pieces (page 125) and cut out.
- Iron fabric stabilizer onto the back of the fabrics.
- Trace the patterns onto the fabrics and cut out.

Instructions

Hands

STEP 1

Fold each hand piece in half horizontally (see pattern); stitch around the shape.

Feet

STEP 2

Glue the front and back leg/foot pieces together and stitch around each shape. Fold the foot forward (see pattern) and press.

Sleeves

STEP 3

Roll each sleeve piece in half, slipstitch together. Fill with stuffing. Put a hand into each sleeve. Stitch the sleeve and hands together, stitching sleeve end closed. Attach each sleeve onto the body base at the shoulders, closing sleeve end (Figure A).

Jabot

STEP 4

Accordion fold the jabot piece.

Order of Application

STEP 5

Apply a dot of glue to the wrong side of the small pieces and affix in the following order: body base front (with attached arms), feet (ends overlap the body base by ¼" (0.6 cm)), pants, shirt center, sash, short hanging sash, long hanging sash, face, bandana, eye patch, jabot.

STEP 6

Stitch around each piece with matching thread. Glue the body base back onto the front body, wrong sides facing. Cut out any parts of the body base that show at the sides of the doll parts. Stitch around the entire shape base shape with matching thread.

Embellishments

STEP 7

Embroider the eye, mouth, stripes on the bandana, and line between the legs.

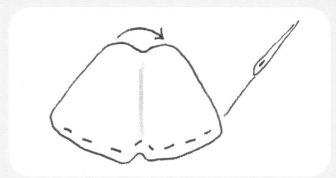

Figure A

Pretty Pirate

MATERIALS

- Felt:
  - Black (body base front/back, hat, skirt): 6" x 6½" (15 cm x 16 cm)
  - White (sleeves, shirt, neck ruffle): 4" x 5½" (10 cm x 14 cm)
  - Red (waist band, skirt top x 2): 2" x 4" (5 cm x 10 cm)
  - Skin-color felt (head, hands, legs): 3" x 3½" (8 cm x 9 cm)
  - Skin-color, red, black, white and blue thread
- Brown embroidery thread
- Black iron-on fabric stabilizer: 4½" x 6½" (11 cm x 16 cm)
- Fabric glue
- Poly fiberfill stuffing for sleeves
- White acrylic paint
- Small paint brush
- Tiny feather

Getting Started

11 pattern pieces

- Copy the pattern pieces (page 126) and cut out.
- Iron black fabric stabilizer onto the back of all fabrics.
- Trace the pattern pieces onto the fabric and cut out.

Instructions

Hands

STEP 1

Fold each hand piece in half horizontally (see pattern), stitch around the shape.

Sleeves

STEP 2

Gather both bottom ends of each sleeve piece (see pattern). Roll each sleeve piece and fill with stuffing; slipstitch closed along bottom (Figure A).

STEP 3

Insert a hand into the gathered end of each sleeve; stitch together, closing the sleeve end. Stitch each sleeve onto the shoulder area of the shirt piece.

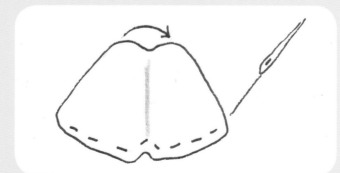

Figure A

Collar

STEP 4

Accordion fold the neck ruffle; press.

Skirt

STEP 5

Gather the top of the skirt and skirt top pieces (see pattern). Glue one skirt top piece onto each side of the skirt, at the top (Figure B).

Hair

STEP 6

Cut brown embroidery thread into six 2½" (6 cm) pieces. Divide the pieces into 3 groups (2 strands in each group). Tie a knot at one end, braid the strands together, then tie a knot at the other end. Tie a piece of red thread around the bottom of the braid. Repeat to make the second braid. When assembling the doll, place one braid on either side of the face, and tuck the tops of the braids under the edge of the hat.

Order of Application

STEP 7

Apply a dot of glue to the wrong side of the small pieces and affix in the following order: body base front, legs, skirt/top skirts, head, braids, shirt (with attached arms), neck ruffle, waistband, hat.

STEP 8

Stitch around each piece with matching thread. Glue the back body onto the front body, wrong sides facing. Cut out any parts of the body base that show at the sides of the doll parts. Stitch around the entire base shape with matching thread.

Embellishments

STEP 9

Embroider the eyes, mouth and line between the legs.

STEP 10

Glue a tiny feather in the hat.

STEP 11

Paint a skull and crossbones on the hat with a very small brush and white acrylic paint.

Figure B

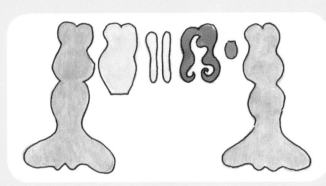

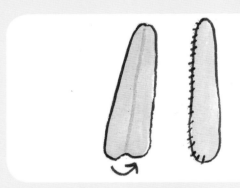

Figure A

Mermaid

MATERIALS

- Felt:
    - Turquoise (body base): 6" x 6½" (15 cm x 16 cm)
    - Skin-color (upper body, arms): 2" x 5½" (5 cm x 14 cm)
    - Green (scales): 2" x 3" (5 cm x 8 cm)
    - Orange (hair): 2" x 2½" (5 cm x 6 cm)
- White iron-on fabric stabilizer: 6" x 6½" (15 cm x 16 cm)
- Orange, skin-color, turquoise, green and red thread
- Fabric glue
- Turquoise marker

Getting Started

5 pattern pieces

- Copy the pattern pieces (page 127) and cut out.
- Iron fabric stabilizer onto the back of all fabrics.
- Trace the pattern pieces onto the fabrics and cut out.

Instructions

Arms

STEP 1

Fold each arm piece in half vertically (see pattern), slipstitch the shape together (Figure A). Stitch each arm to the upper body piece at the shoulder.

Body

STEP 2

Glue scales onto bottom of body base front.

Order of Application

STEP 3

Apply a dot of glue to the wrong side of the small pieces and affix in the following order: body base front (with scales), upper body (with attached arms), hair.

STEP 4

Stitch around each piece with matching thread. Glue the back body onto the front body, wrong sides facing. Stitch around the entire shape with matching thread. If there is any fabric stabilizer visible on the sides, color with the turquoise marker. If there is any blue fabric showing around the upper body, cut it off.

Embellishments

STEP 5

Embroider eyes and a mouth.

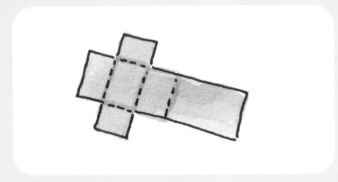

Treasure Chest

MATERIALS

- Brown felt: 5" x 13½" (13 cm x 35 cm)
- Black iron-on fabric stabilizer: 5" x 13½" (13 cm x 35 cm)
- Brown and yellow ochre thread
- Fabric glue
- Gold trim: 15" (38 cm)
- Faux gold coins, jewels and beads, old coins

Getting Started

2 pattern pieces

- Copy the pattern pieces (page 128) and cut out.
- Iron fabric stabilizer onto the back of the fabric.
- Trace the pattern pieces onto the fabric and cut out.

Instructions

STEP 1

Fold up the four sides of one base piece (see pattern), right sides out; press. As you fold up each side piece, sew it to the abutting piece with blanket stitch (Figures A and B).

STEP 2

Bring up the lid; stitch together the corners with blanket stitch.

STEP 3

Pin one lid end piece along one side of the lid (Figure C); stitch together with blanket stitch. Do this at both ends.

STEP 4

Repeat steps 1 to 3 to make a second chest shape, this time, with right sides in. (One chest will have the brown side of the fabric facing out; the other will have the brown side of the fabric facing in.)

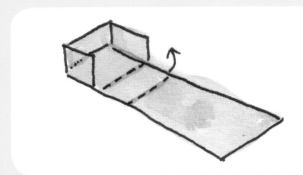

Figure A

Figure B

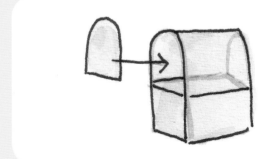

Figure C

STEP 5

Apply glue all over the inside of the outer chest and push the inner chest into it, wrong sides facing (Figure D).

STEP 6

Stitch together along the edges with blanket stitch.

STEP 7

Glue trim on the outside of the chest (see pattern) (Figure E). Fill with faux gold coins, jewels and beads.

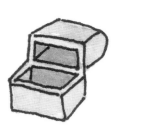

Figure D

Figure E

Patterns
Little Ballerina Ballet Bag Pattern
PHOTOCOPY PATTERNS BY 250%

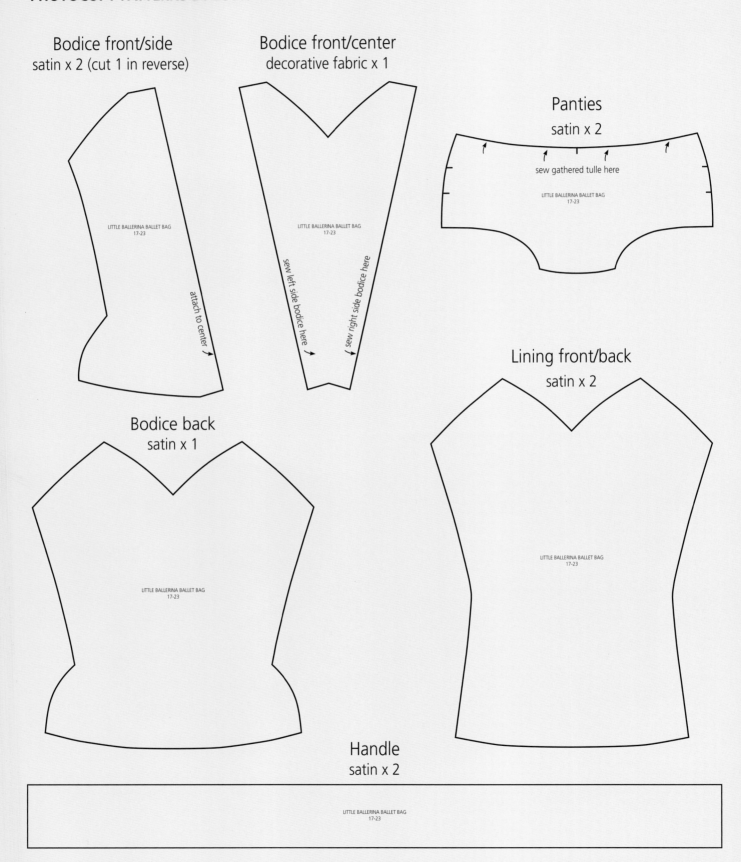

Bodice front/side
satin x 2 (cut 1 in reverse)

Bodice front/center
decorative fabric x 1

Panties
satin x 2

sew gathered tulle here

LITTLE BALLERINA BALLET BAG
17-23

attach to center

sew left side bodice here

sew right side bodice here

Bodice back
satin x 1

LITTLE BALLERINA BALLET BAG
17-23

Lining front/back
satin x 2

LITTLE BALLERINA BALLET BAG
17-23

LITTLE BALLERINA BALLET BAG
17-23

Handle
satin x 2

LITTLE BALLERINA BALLET BAG
17-23

Fear the Kraken! Pattern

PHOTOCOPY PATTERNS BY 400%

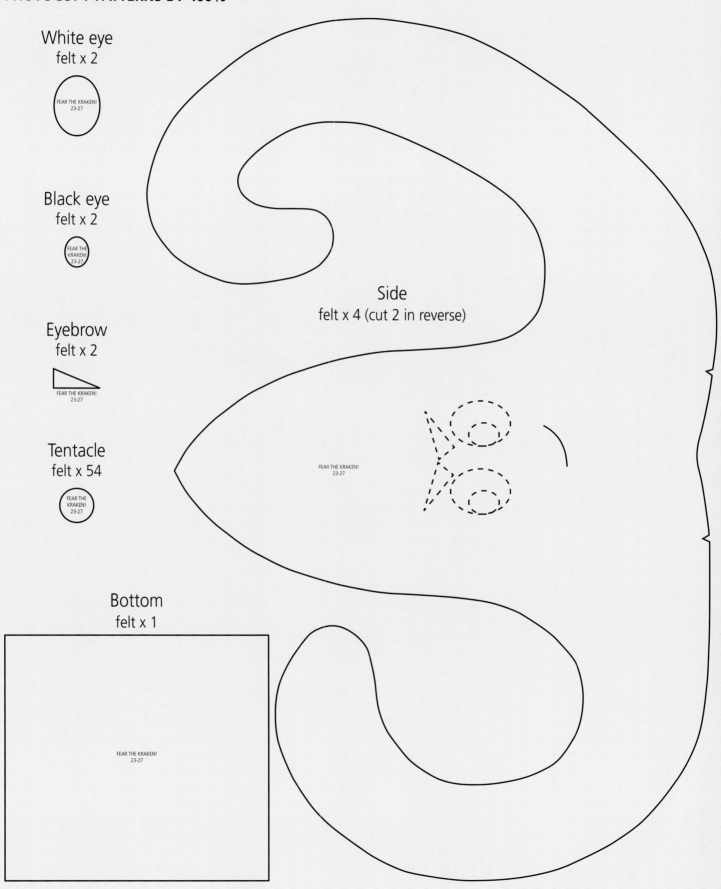

White eye
felt x 2

Black eye
felt x 2

Eyebrow
felt x 2

Tentacle
felt x 54

Bottom
felt x 1

Side
felt x 4 (cut 2 in reverse)

Superhero Cape and Mask Pattern

PHOTOCOPY PATTERNS BY 400%

Actual cape length: 36" (91 cm)

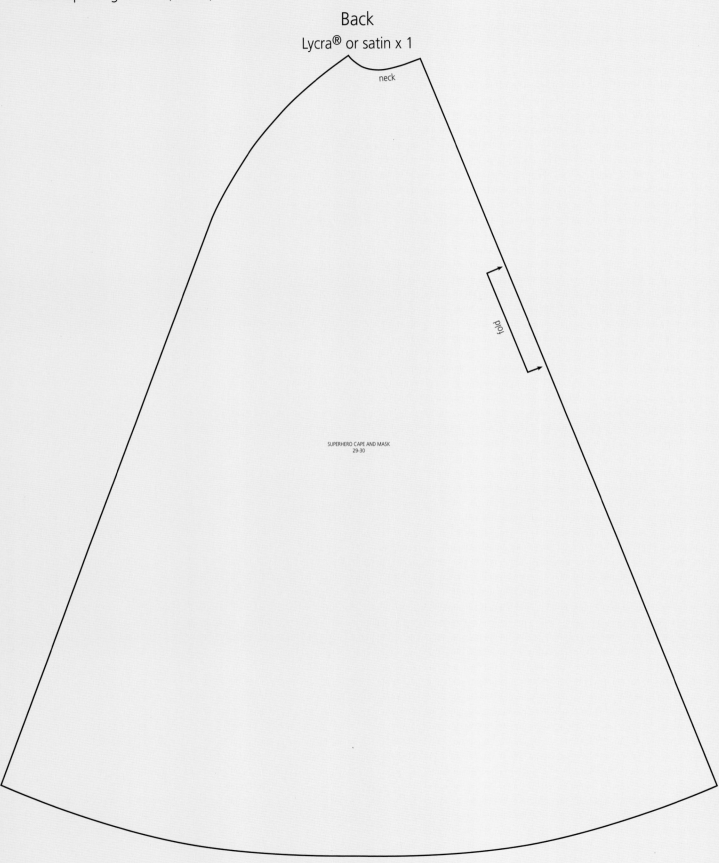

Back

Lycra® or satin x 1

neck

fold

SUPERHERO CAPE AND MASK
29-30

Mask
Lycra® or satin x 1

SUPERHERO CAPE AND MASK
29-30

cut out   cut out

Sides
Lycra® or satin x 2 (cut 1 in reverse)

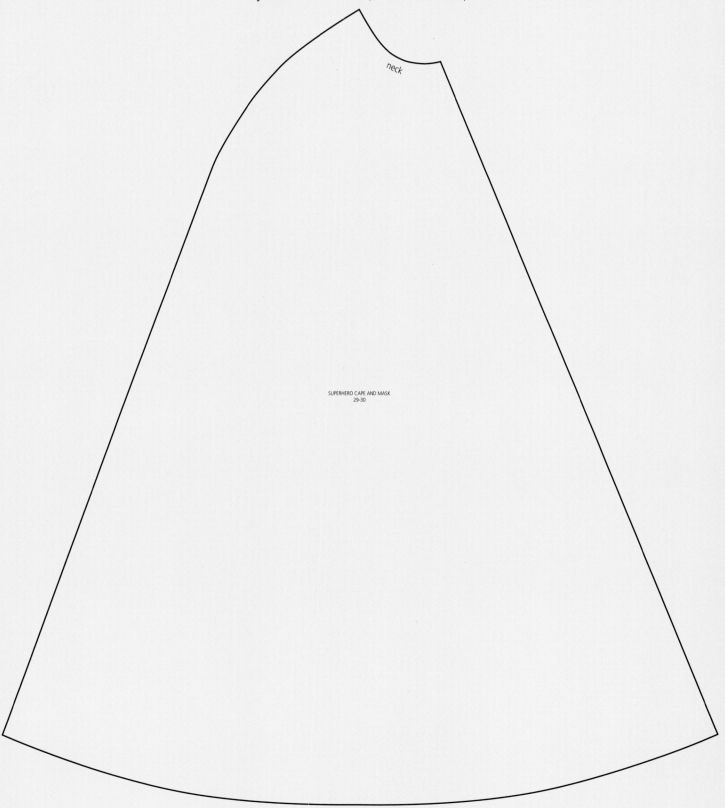

neck

SUPERHERO CAPE AND MASK
29-30

Ahoy! It's a Pirate Hat Pattern

PHOTOCOPY PATTERNS BY 250%

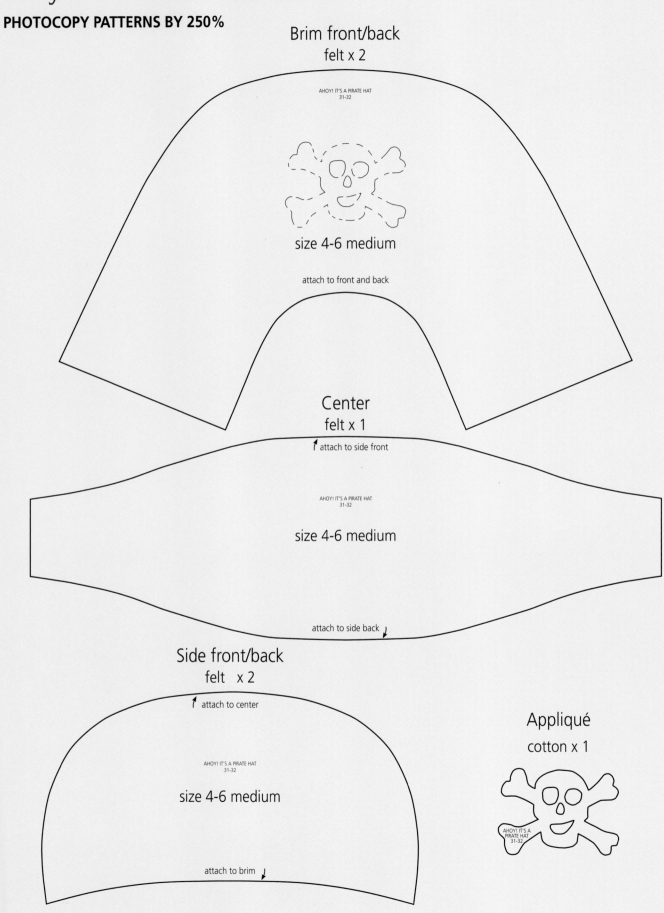

Brim front/back
felt x 2

AHOY! IT'S A PIRATE HAT
31-32

size 4-6 medium

attach to front and back

Center
felt x 1

attach to side front

AHOY! IT'S A PIRATE HAT
31-32

size 4-6 medium

attach to side back

Side front/back
felt   x 2

attach to center

AHOY! IT'S A PIRATE HAT
31-32

size 4-6 medium

attach to brim

Appliqué
cotton x 1

AHOY! IT'S A
PIRATE HAT
31-32

Jolly Roger Pirate Flag Pattern

PHOTOCOPY PATTERNS BY 400%

Skull and crossbones appliqué

felt x 1

Bandana appliqué

cotton or felt x 1

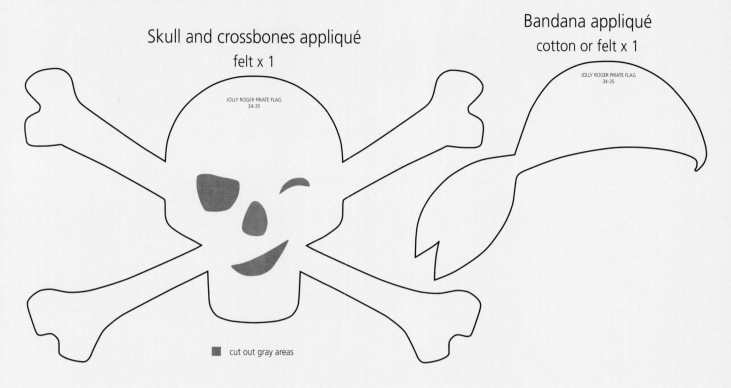

cut out gray areas

Flag front/back

felt x 2

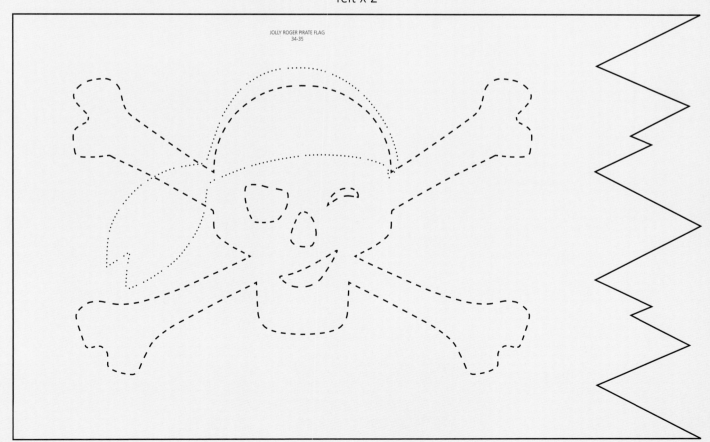

Excalibur Sword Pattern

PHOTOCOPY PATTERNS BY 400%

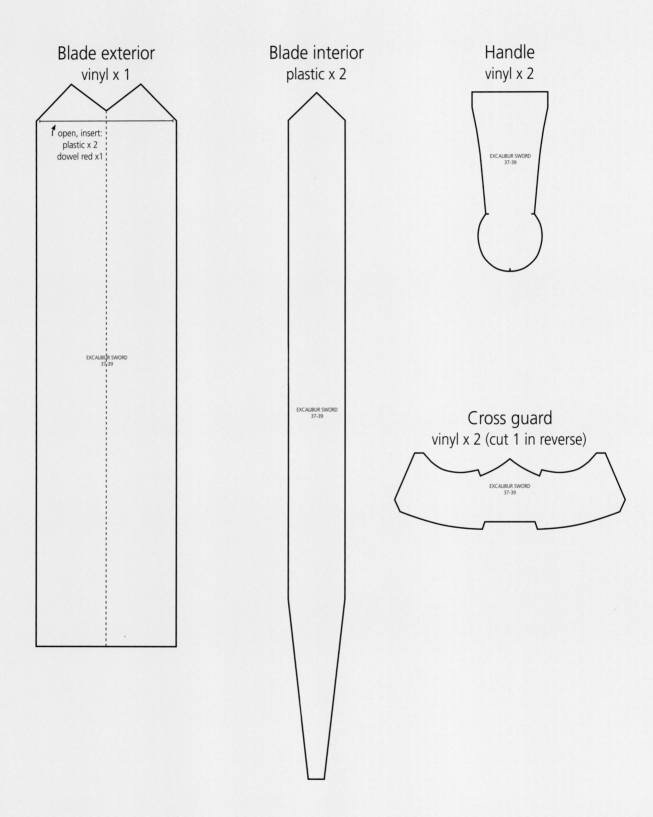

Blade exterior
vinyl x 1

open, insert:
plastic x 2
dowel red x1

EXCALIBUR SWORD
37-39

Blade interior
plastic x 2

EXCALIBUR SWORD
37-39

Handle
vinyl x 2

EXCALIBUR SWORD
37-39

Cross guard
vinyl x 2 (cut 1 in reverse)

EXCALIBUR SWORD
37-39

Noble Knight's Hood Pattern

PHOTOCOPY PATTERNS BY 200%

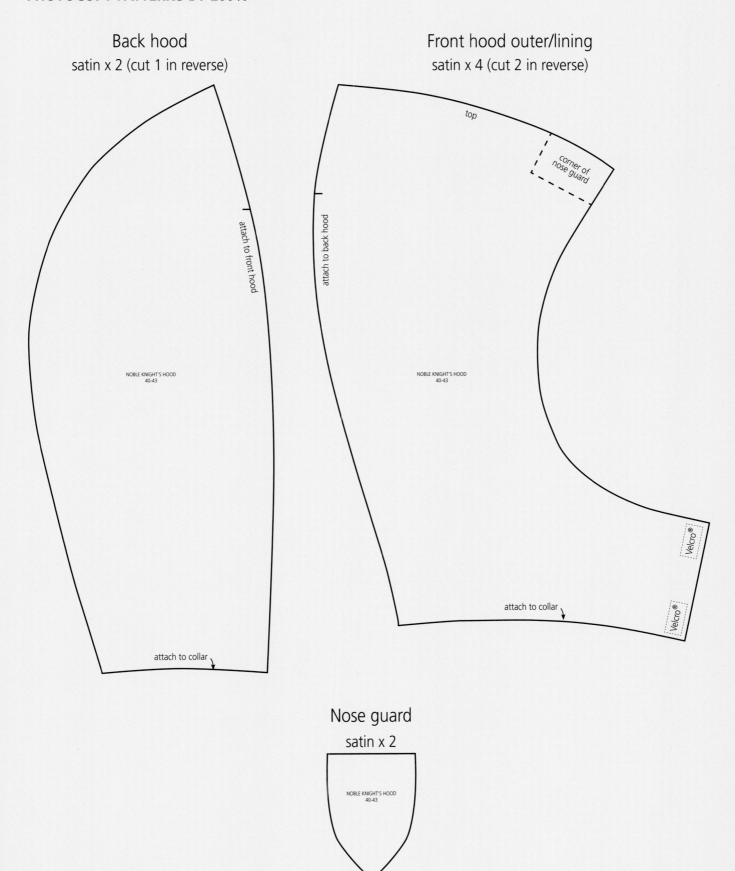

Back hood
satin x 2 (cut 1 in reverse)

Front hood outer/lining
satin x 4 (cut 2 in reverse)

top

corner of nose guard

attach to front hood

attach to back hood

NOBLE KNIGHT'S HOOD
40-43

NOBLE KNIGHT'S HOOD
40-43

Velcro®

Velcro®

attach to collar

attach to collar

Nose guard

satin x 2

NOBLE KNIGHT'S HOOD
40-43

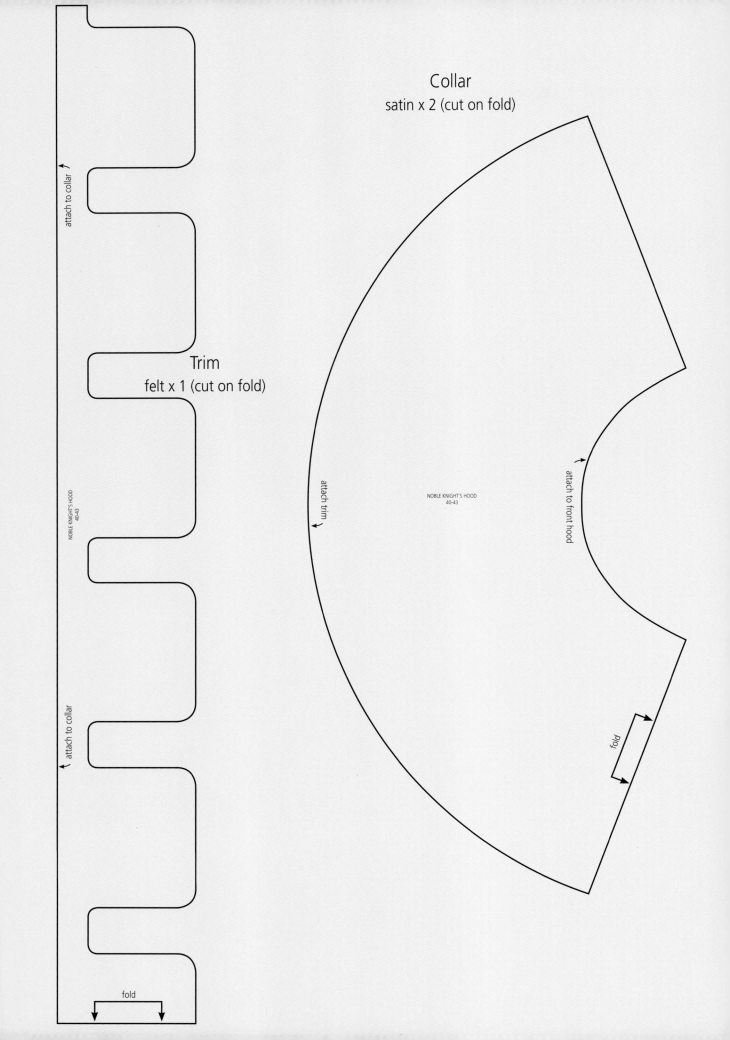

Collar
satin x 2 (cut on fold)

attach to collar

Trim
felt x 1 (cut on fold)

NOBLE KNIGHT'S HOOD
40-43

attach to collar

fold

attach trim

NOBLE KNIGHT'S HOOD
40-43

attach to front hood

fold

A Royal Crown Pattern

PHOTOCOPY PATTERNS BY 400%

Crown front/back
decorative fabric x 1
lining x 1

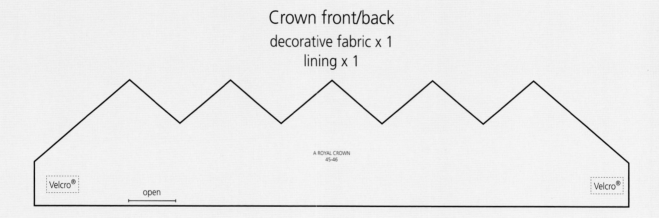

Broomstick Stallion Pattern

PHOTOCOPY PATTERNS BY 250%

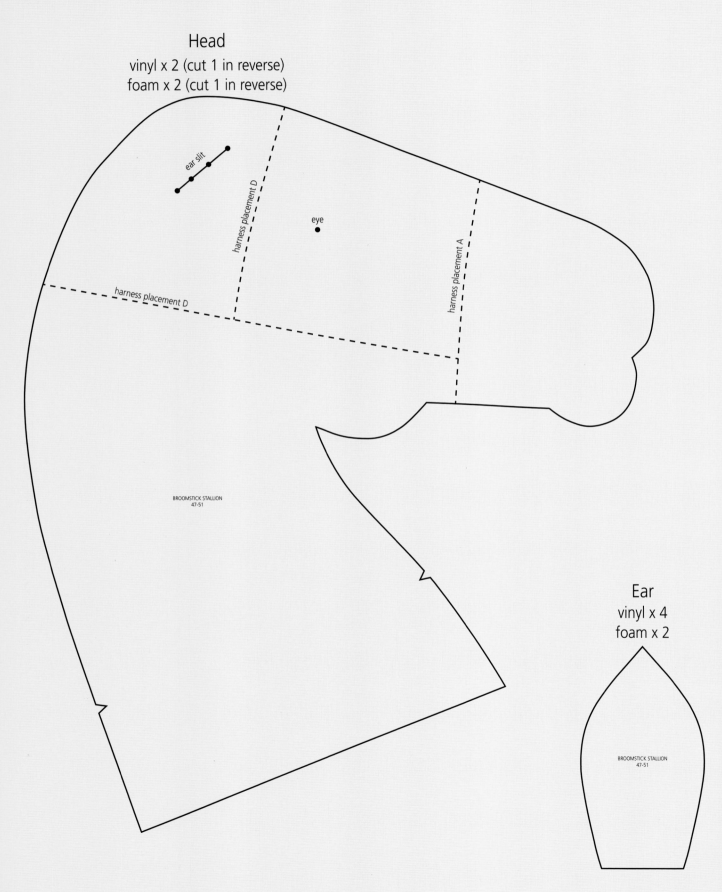

Head
vinyl x 2 (cut 1 in reverse)
foam x 2 (cut 1 in reverse)

ear slit

harness placement D

eye

harness placement A

harness placement D

BROOMSTICK STALLION
47-51

Ear
vinyl x 4
foam x 2

BROOMSTICK STALLION
47-51

My Very Own Baby Doll Pattern

PHOTOCOPY PATTERNS BY 200%

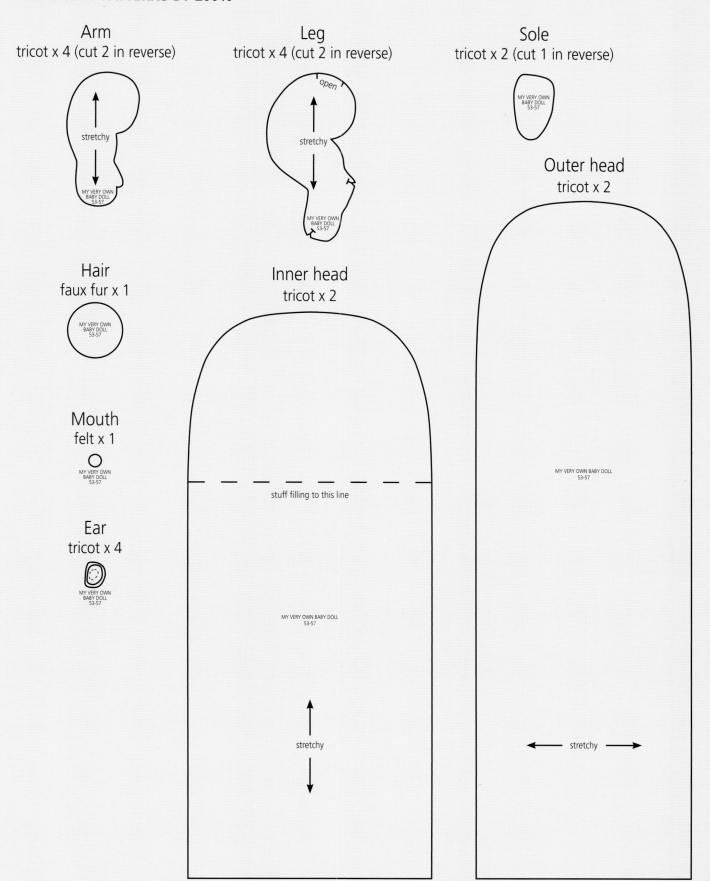

Arm
tricot x 4 (cut 2 in reverse)

stretchy

MY VERY OWN BABY DOLL 53-57

Leg
tricot x 4 (cut 2 in reverse)

open

stretchy

MY VERY OWN BABY DOLL 53-57

Sole
tricot x 2 (cut 1 in reverse)

MY VERY OWN BABY DOLL 53-57

Outer head
tricot x 2

MY VERY OWN BABY DOLL 53-57

stretchy

Hair
faux fur x 1

MY VERY OWN BABY DOLL 53-57

Inner head
tricot x 2

stuff filling to this line

MY VERY OWN BABY DOLL 53-57

stretchy

Mouth
felt x 1

MY VERY OWN BABY DOLL 53-57

Ear
tricot x 4

MY VERY OWN BABY DOLL 53-57

Doll Clothes Pattern

PHOTOCOPY PATTERNS BY 250%

Bodice front
cotton x 1

neck

arm hole

arm hole

DOLL CLOTHES
59-65

waist

Sleeve
cotton x 2 (cut 1 in reverse)

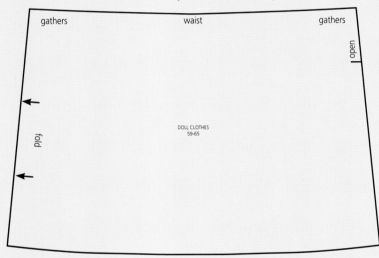

shoulder

DOLL CLOTHES
59-65

hem edge

Bodice back
cotton x 2 (cut 1 in reverse)

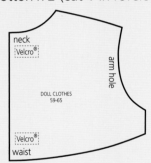

neck

Velcro®

arm hole

DOLL CLOTHES
59-65

Velcro®

waist

Skirt
cotton x 2 (cut 1 in reverse)

gathers

waist

gathers

open

fold

DOLL CLOTHES
59-65

Bonnet back
cotton x 1

DOLL CLOTHES
59-65

Bonnet brim
cotton x 1

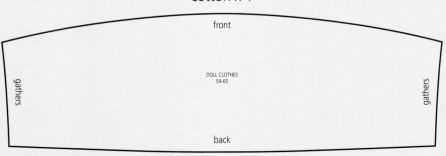

front

gathers

gathers

DOLL CLOTHES
59-65

back

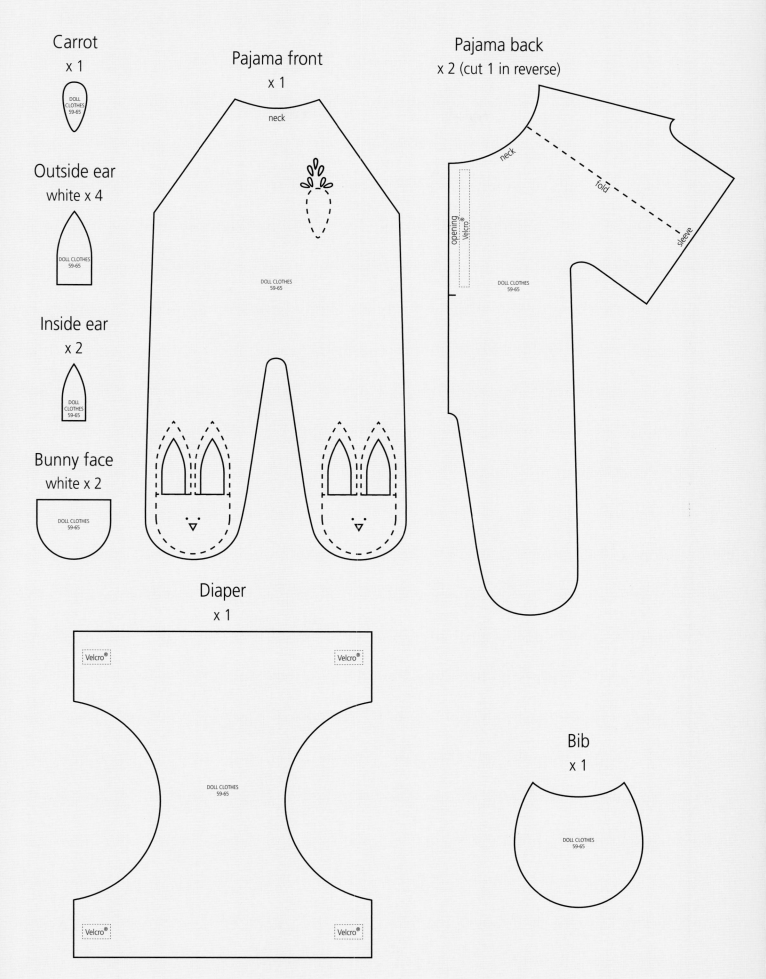

Carrot
x 1

Pajama front
x 1

Pajama back
x 2 (cut 1 in reverse)

neck

DOLL CLOTHES
59-65

neck

opening
Velcro®

fold

sleeve

DOLL CLOTHES
59-65

Outside ear
white x 4

DOLL CLOTHES
59-65

Inside ear
x 2

DOLL CLOTHES
59-65

Bunny face
white x 2

DOLL CLOTHES
59-65

neck

DOLL CLOTHES
59-65

Diaper
x 1

Velcro®   Velcro®

DOLL CLOTHES
59-65

Velcro®   Velcro®

Bib
x 1

DOLL CLOTHES
59-65

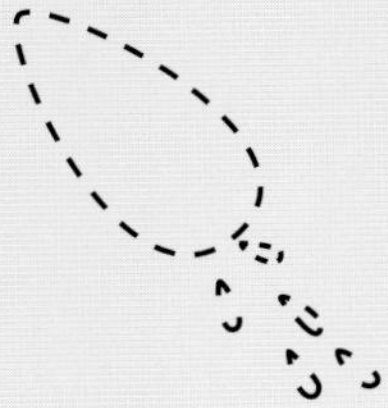

Blanket

x 1

DOLL CLOTHES
59-65

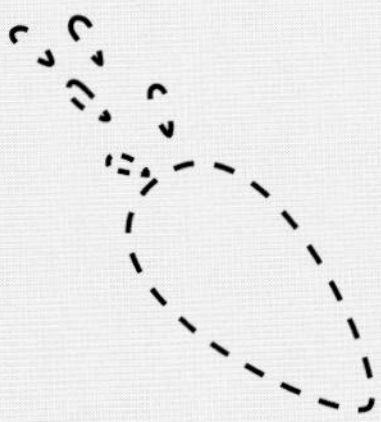

Pop Star Microphone Pattern

PHOTOCOPY PATTERNS BY 100%

Handle
satin x 4

↑ attach to top

POP STAR MICROPHONE
67-69

Top
knit x 4

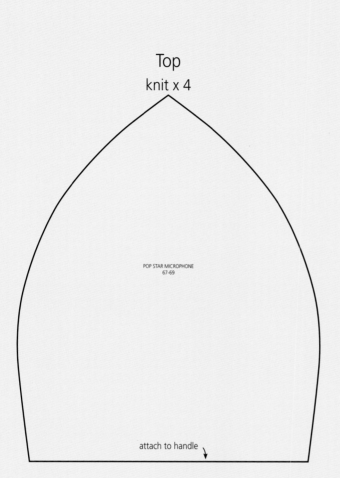

POP STAR MICROPHONE
67-69

attach to handle ↘

Bottom
satin x 1

POP STAR MICROPHONE
67-69

My Favorite Mermaid Pattern

PHOTOCOPY PATTERNS BY 200%

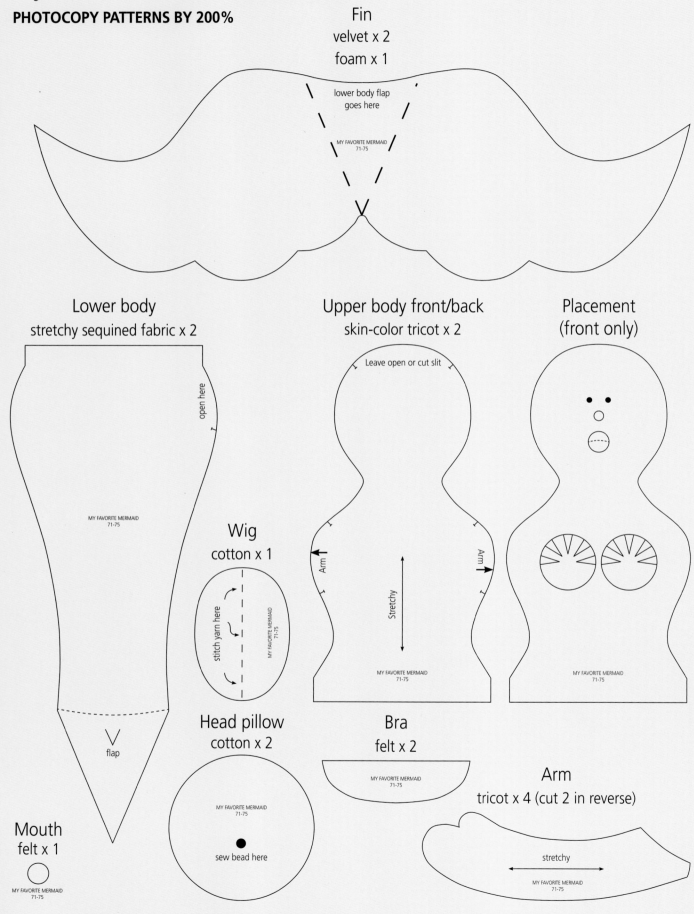

Fin
velvet x 2
foam x 1

lower body flap
goes here

MY FAVORITE MERMAID
71-75

Lower body
stretchy sequined fabric x 2

open here

MY FAVORITE MERMAID
71-75

V
flap

Upper body front/back
skin-color tricot x 2

Leave open or cut slit

Arm

Arm

Stretchy

MY FAVORITE MERMAID
71-75

Placement
(front only)

MY FAVORITE MERMAID
71-75

Wig
cotton x 1

stitch yarn here

MY FAVORITE MERMAID
71-75

Head pillow
cotton x 2

MY FAVORITE MERMAID
71-75

sew bead here

Bra
felt x 2

MY FAVORITE MERMAID
71-75

Arm
tricot x 4 (cut 2 in reverse)

stretchy

MY FAVORITE MERMAID
71-75

Mouth
felt x 1

MY FAVORITE MERMAID
71-75

118

Handy Dandy Tool Belt and Tools Pattern

PHOTOCOPY PATTERNS BY 250%

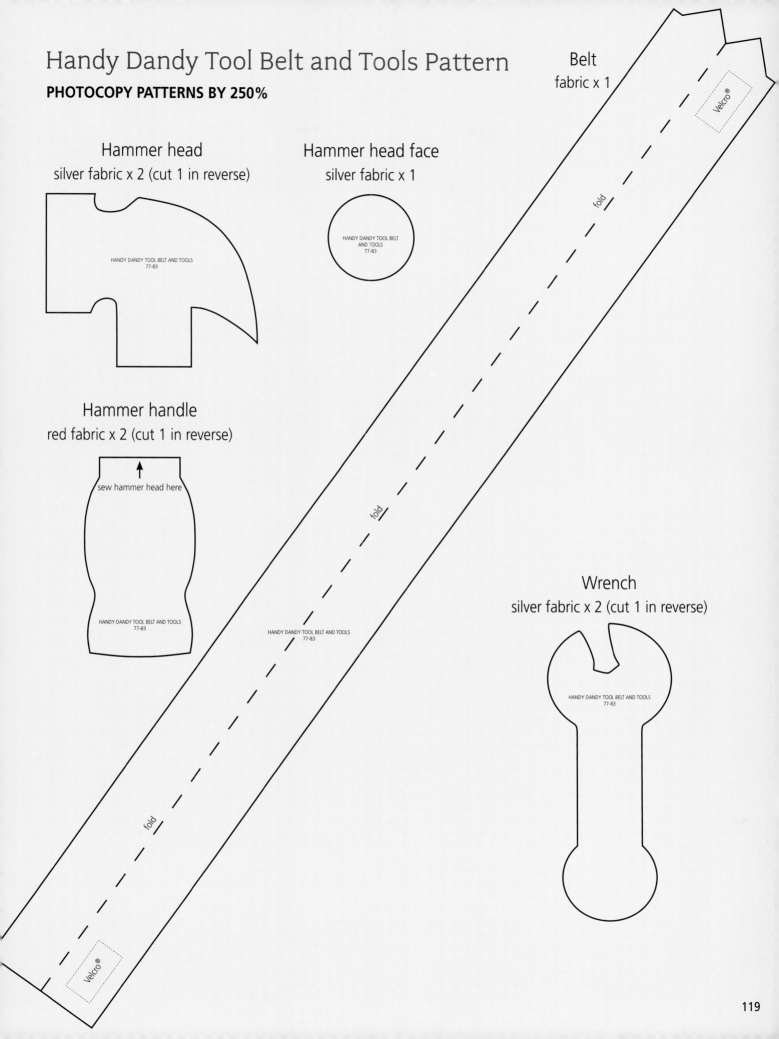

Hammer head
silver fabric x 2 (cut 1 in reverse)

HANDY DANDY TOOL BELT AND TOOLS
77-83

Hammer head face
silver fabric x 1

HANDY DANDY TOOL BELT
AND TOOLS
77-83

Belt
fabric x 1

Velcro®

fold

Hammer handle
red fabric x 2 (cut 1 in reverse)

sew hammer head here

HANDY DANDY TOOL BELT AND TOOLS
77-83

fold

HANDY DANDY TOOL BELT AND TOOLS
77-83

fold

Velcro®

Wrench
silver fabric x 2 (cut 1 in reverse)

HANDY DANDY TOOL BELT AND TOOLS
77-83

Saw handle
blue fabric x 2 (cut 1 in reverse)

insert saw here

HANDY DANDY TOOL BELT AND TOOLS
77-83

Outer blade
silver fabric x 2 (cut 1 in reverse)

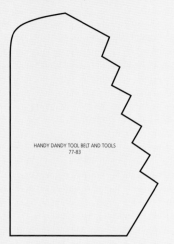

HANDY DANDY TOOL BELT AND TOOLS
77-83

Inner blade
foam x 2
plastic x 1

HANDY DANDY TOOL BELT AND TOOLS
77-83

Screwdriver head
silver fabric x 2 (cut 1 in reverse)

HANDY DANDY TOOL BELT
AND TOOLS
77-83

Screwdriver handle
yellow fabric x 2

HANDY DANDY TOOL BELT AND TOOLS
77-83

Tool pouch
fabric x 2

Side loop
fabric x 2

HANDY DANDY TOOL BELT AND TOOLS
77-83

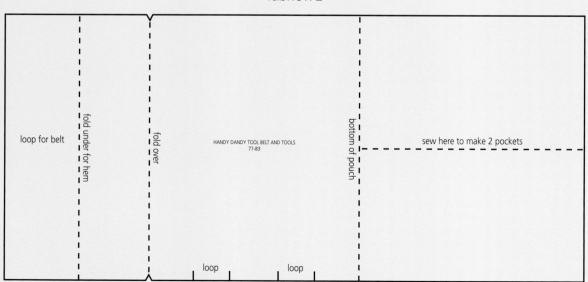

loop for belt

fold under for hem

fold over

HANDY DANDY TOOL BELT AND TOOLS
77-83

bottom of pouch

sew here to make 2 pockets

loop   loop

Plundering Pirate Ship Pattern

PHOTOCOPY PATTERNS BY 250%

Outer ship sides
brown fabric x 2 (cut 1 in reverse)
foam x 2

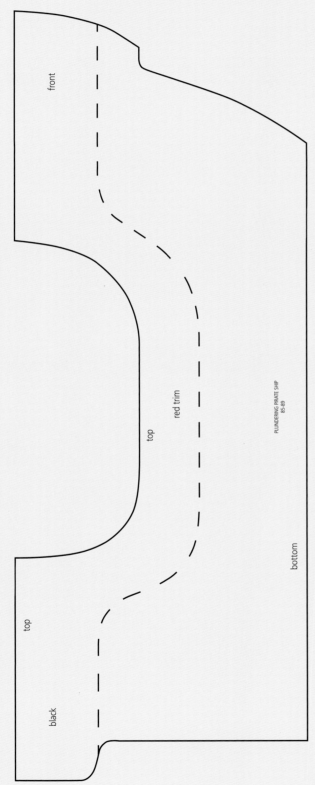

Inner ship sides
yellow fabric x 2 (cut 1 in reverse)
foam x 2 (cut 1 in reverse)

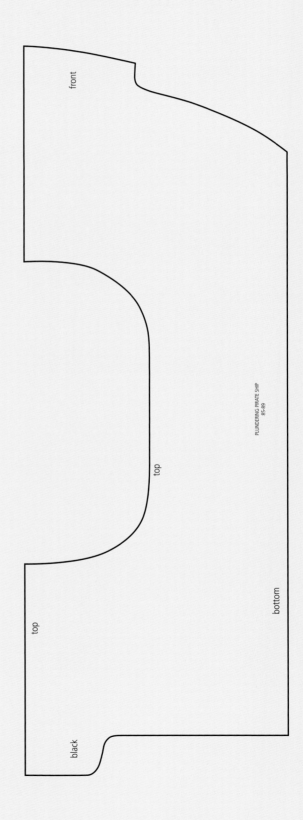

Side trim
red fabric x 2 (cut 1 in reverse)

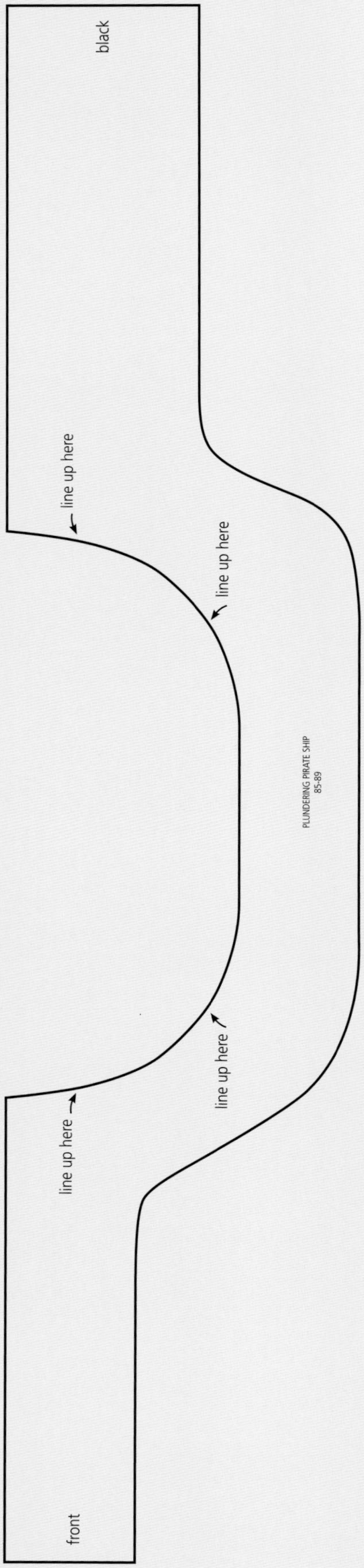

black

line up here

line up here

PLUNDERING PIRATE SHIP
85-89

line up here

line up here

line up here

front

Outer ship bottom
brown fabric x 1
foam x 1

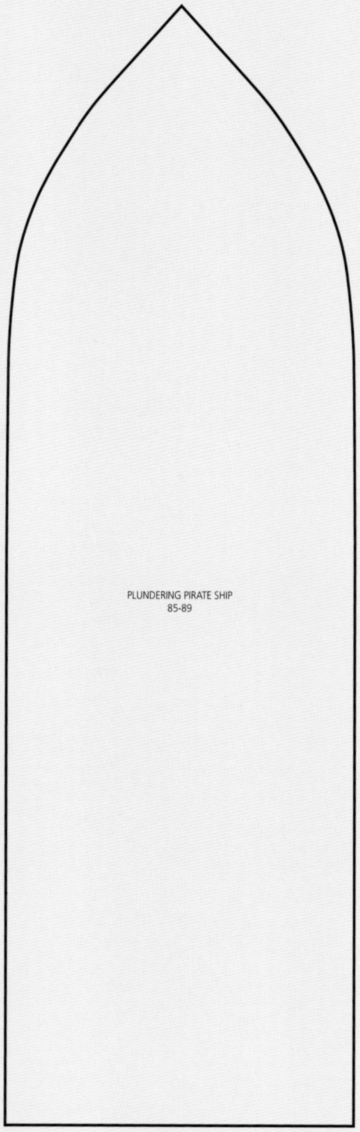

PLUNDERING PIRATE SHIP
85-89

Mast support
foam x 2

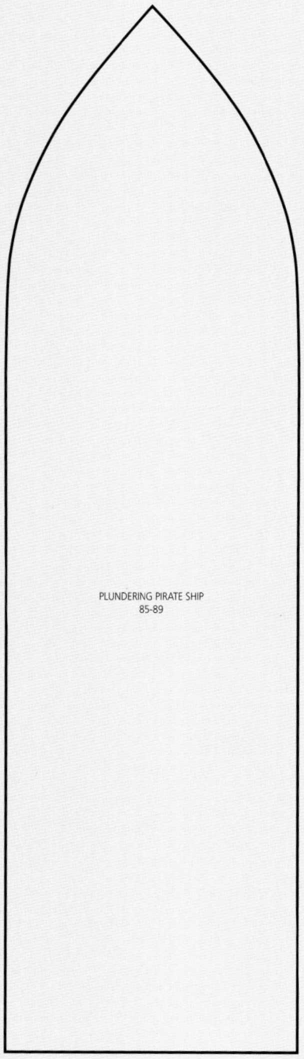

PLUNDERING PIRATE SHIP
85-89

Inner ship bottom
yellow fabric x 2
foam x 1

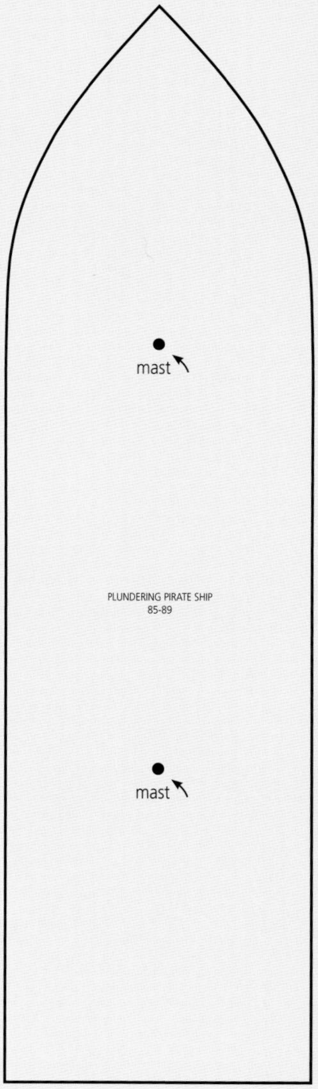

mast

mast

PLUNDERING PIRATE SHIP
85-89

Small sail front/back
white fabric x 4

PLUNDERING PIRATE SHIP
85-89

Large sail front/back
white fabric x 4

PLUNDERING PIRATE SHIP
85-89

Flag
black felt x 2

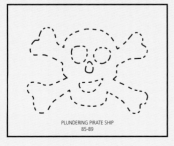

PLUNDERING PIRATE SHIP
85-89

Appliqué
white felt x 1

PLUNDERING
PIRATE SHIP
85-89

■ cut out gray areas

Back trim
red fabric x 1

PLUNDERING PIRATE SHIP
85-89

Inner ship end
yellow fabric x 1
foam x 1

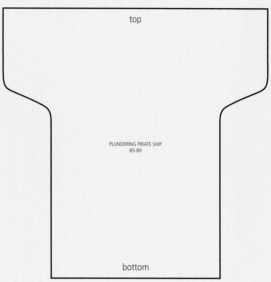

top

PLUNDERING PIRATE SHIP
85-89

bottom

Outer ship end
brown fabric x 1
foam x 1

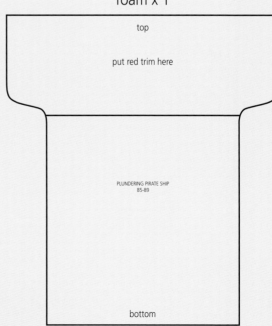

top

put red trim here

PLUNDERING PIRATE SHIP
85-89

bottom

Pirate Ship Dolls and Treasure Chest Pattern

PHOTOCOPY PATTERNS BY 100%

Captain

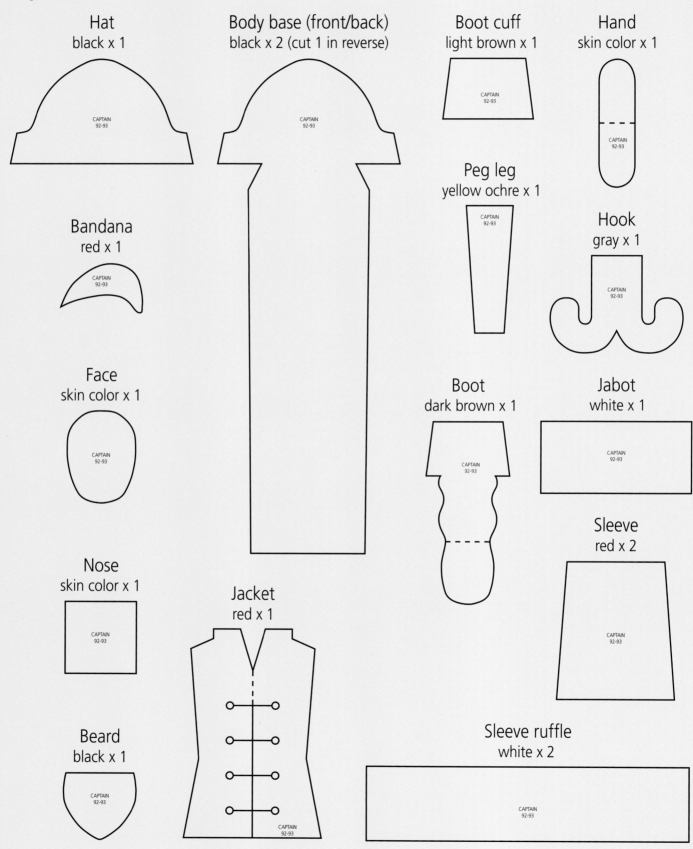

Hat
black x 1

Body base (front/back)
black x 2 (cut 1 in reverse)

Boot cuff
light brown x 1

Hand
skin color x 1

Peg leg
yellow ochre x 1

Bandana
red x 1

Hook
gray x 1

Face
skin color x 1

Boot
dark brown x 1

Jabot
white x 1

Sleeve
red x 2

Nose
skin color x 1

Jacket
red x 1

Beard
black x 1

Sleeve ruffle
white x 2

First Mate

Bandana
red x 1

Face
skin color x 1

Eye patch
black x 1

Hand
skin color x 1

Foot
skin color x 4

Body base (front/back)
brown x 2

Pants
yellow ochre x 1

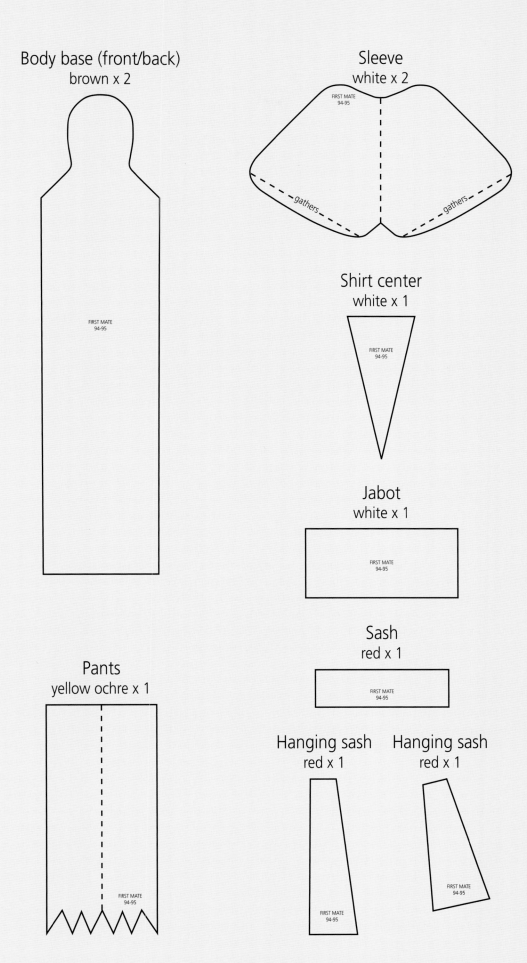

Sleeve
white x 2

gathers   gathers

Shirt center
white x 1

Jabot
white x 1

Sash
red x 1

Hanging sash
red x 1

Hanging sash
red x 1

FIRST MATE 94-95

Pretty Pirate

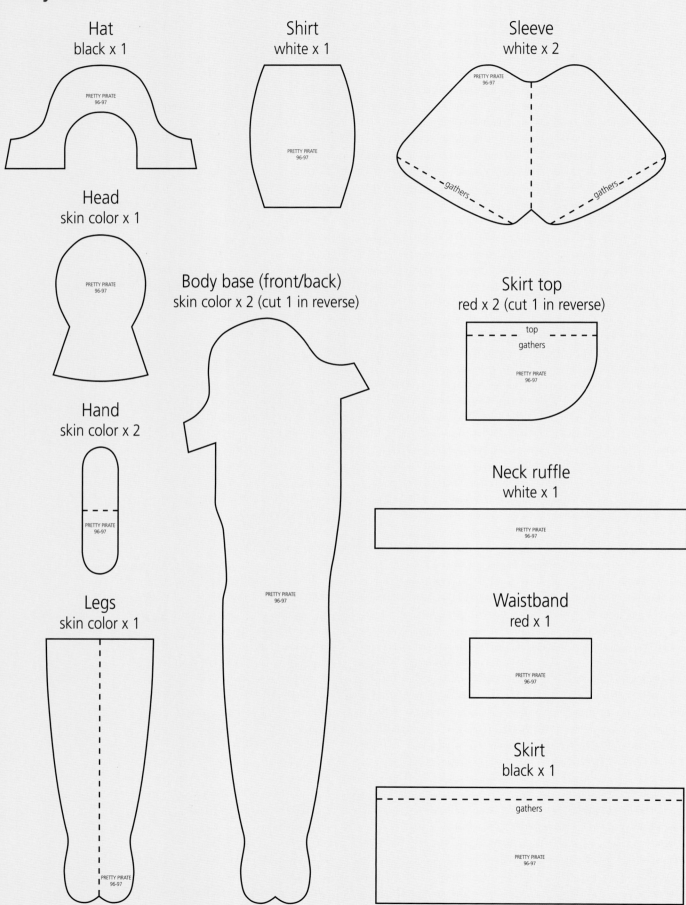

Hat
black x 1

PRETTY PIRATE
96-97

Shirt
white x 1

PRETTY PIRATE
96-97

Sleeve
white x 2

PRETTY PIRATE
96-97

gathers

gathers

Head
skin color x 1

PRETTY PIRATE
96-97

Body base (front/back)
skin color x 2 (cut 1 in reverse)

PRETTY PIRATE
96-97

Skirt top
red x 2 (cut 1 in reverse)

top

gathers

PRETTY PIRATE
96-97

Hand
skin color x 2

PRETTY PIRATE
96-97

Neck ruffle
white x 1

PRETTY PIRATE
96-97

Waistband
red x 1

PRETTY PIRATE
96-97

Legs
skin color x 1

PRETTY PIRATE
96-97

Skirt
black x 1

gathers

PRETTY PIRATE
96-97

Mermaid

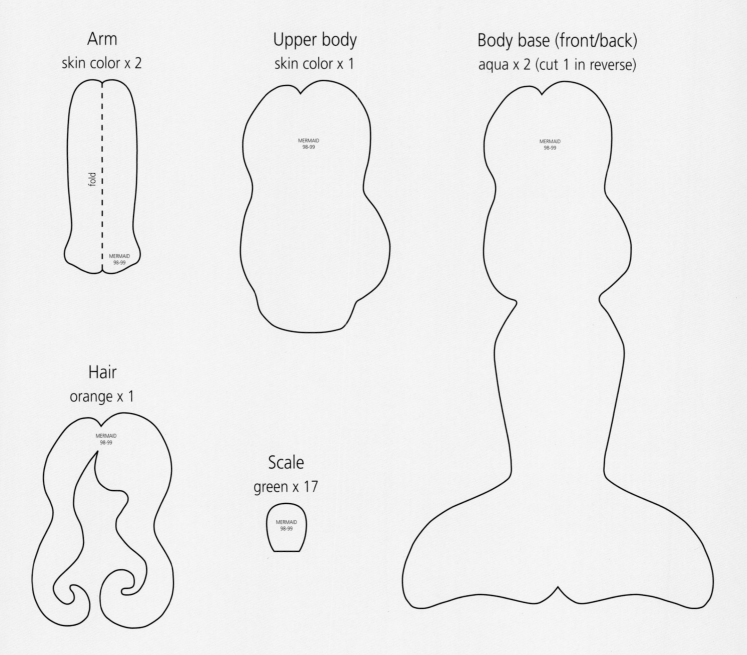

Arm
skin color x 2

MERMAID
98-99

Upper body
skin color x 1

MERMAID
98-99

Body base (front/back)
aqua x 2 (cut 1 in reverse)

MERMAID
98-99

Hair
orange x 1

MERMAID
98-99

Scale
green x 17

MERMAID
98-99

Treasure Chest

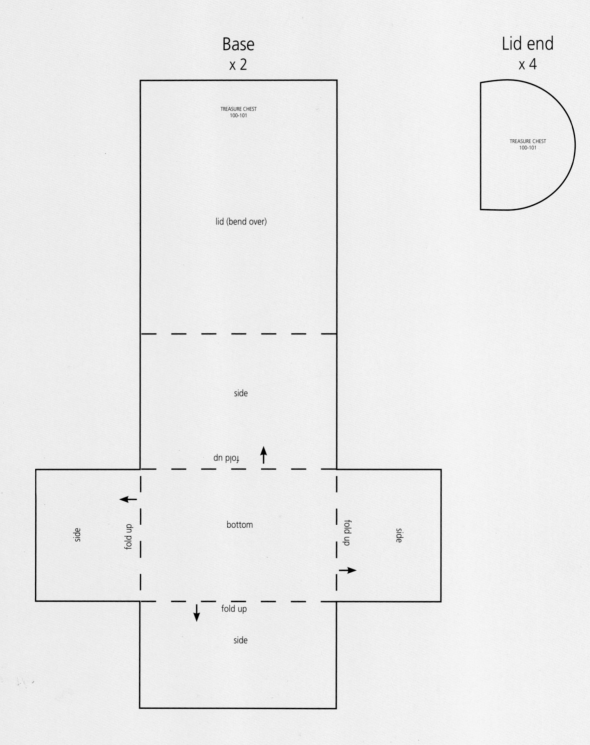

Base
x 2

TREASURE CHEST
100-101

lid (bend over)

side

fold up ↑

side   fold up ←   bottom   fold up   side

fold up →

fold up ↓

side

Lid end
x 4

TREASURE CHEST
100-101